# RAF BIGGIN HILL
# 1939 - 1940

# RAF BIGGIN HILL
# 1939 – 1940

The Aerodrome's role from the outbreak of WW2,
the Battle of France, Dunkirk and
Battle of Britain

**Richard C. Smith**

Mitor Publications

Published & typeset by
Mitor Publications
20 Theydon Gardens,
Rainham,
Essex
RM13 7TU
www.mitorpublications.co.uk



ISBN 9780-9557180-5-2

Cover Design by Ian Taylor
Ian.taylor21@sky.com

Cover image by Barry Weekley
www.barryweekleyart.com



Printed by Martins the Printers Limited
Sea View Works, Spittal, Berwick upon Tweed TD15 1RS
www.martin-the-printers.co.uk

# CONTENTS

# ACKNOWLEDGEMENTS

I would like to thank the following people who helped in many ways to bring about the publication of this book, supplying information and photographs within.

Sincere thanks goes to Colin Brown and Colin Lee for access to their photograph and letter collections. To Christopher Goss MA for allowing use of Luftwaffe photographs from his extensive archive and to Bob Ogley for photographs from his Biggin Hill collection, also Winston Ramsey of After the Battle Publications and No. 610 'County of Chester' Squadron Association for the use of photographs from their archive, also Andy Saunders. Thanks again to Barry Weekley for the excellent painting used for the front cover, and to Ian Taylor for another brilliant book design and photograph section. To the National Archive, Kew, London, the Imperial War Museum Photographic and Sound Archive in Lambeth and the Royal Air Force Museum, Hendon for their help. Thanks to David Brocklehurst MBE, the curator of the Kent Battle of Britain Museum, Hawkinge and the relatives of Siegfried Stronk for their help. Finally to the 'Few' the late Squadron Leader Cyril Bamberger DFC* the late Air Commodore Peter Brothers CBE, DSO, DFC*, the late Group Captain Brian Kingcome DSO, DFC, and Wing Commander Allan Wright DFC* AFC, who gave of their time and wartime memories when interviewed by the author

To Martins the Printers Limited for producing another high quality book once again, many thanks. To my wife Kim and my sons David and Robert for their continuous support and love. Finally to my friends and the general public who continue to support my work.

Richard C. Smith

# INTRODUCTION

Today, Biggin Hill has a successful general-aviation airport running business flights across the United Kingdom and Europe. The airport has its own passenger terminal with departure lounges, a licenced café bar and customs and immigration facilities; however, during the Second World War the aerodrome was one of the most successful fighter stations in RAF Fighter Command, and played a major part in the Battle of Britain.

A number of books have already been written about the history of Biggin Hill's aerodrome over the last sixty years, probably the most notable were RAF Biggin Hill by Graham Wallace in 1957 and more recent 'Biggin on the Bump' and 'Ghosts of Biggin Hill' by Bob Ogley, which covered the aerodromes roll from its early beginnings in 1916 up until 2001.

This book covers the years from 1939 and the outbreak of the Second World War into 1940, when the Nazis invaded Poland Belgium, Holland and France, unleashing their Blitzkrieg on Western Europe and taking control. Also Biggin Hill's role during those desperate days during the Battle of France, sending squadrons to try and quell the German advance. Then the air support over the beaches of Dunkirk as Britain's Royal Navy and the 'Little Ships' tried to get as many of the Allied troops back safely across the Channel during 'Operation Dynamo.'

The aerodrome's greatest challenge was yet to come between July and October 1940, when their pilots took to the air to defend Britain from invasion against the might of the German Luftwaffe who tried to knock out RAF Fighter Command in the air and on the ground and then target London and several other cities.

This book tells of those two years with first-hand accounts by those who served at Biggin Hill and an extensive history using squadron operation records and combat reports as well as new information, never published before.

I hope this book will once again remind future generations of the sacrifice that our countrymen and women paid for our freedom all those years ago.

Richard C. Smith 2015

# Chapter 1
# 1916 – 1938

The story of Biggin Hill started during the summer of 1916, when an alternative site was being reconnoitred by the Royal Flying Corp's Wireless Testing Station, which was then situated at Joyce Green, Kent near the River Thames. They sent two officers to investigate an area between Westerham and Bromley. They travelled to the small village of Aperfield and found 75 acres of flat and well drained ground, but more importantly it was ideally situated for transmission, being one of the highest points in Kent, 600 feet above sea-level.

The decision to locate to this site was approved and by February 1917, the transfer of officers and men had been completed. The new site consisted of canvas tents and wooden huts and one aircraft hangar. The officers were billeted at a large house near to the site which had been requisitioned by the War Office and given over to the Royal Flying Corps. The building known as 'Koonowla' had previously been used as a hospital for sick children.

The first aircraft to land at the new site was an RE7 biplane flown in by Lieutenant Dickie with Air Mechanic Chadwick on a cold snowy day.

During the year of 1917, experimentation of wireless communication between air to ground and air to air continued. After many failures, success was achieved in July 1917, when two Sopwith biplanes flown by Lieutenants Andres and Furnell equipped with helmets and headphones were able to communicate with each other for the first time in aviation history. Major General Sir Hugh Trenchard, Commander of the Royal Flying Corps was highly delighted and so impressed with the work taking place at Biggin, that he instructed that a school of wireless telephony should be set up.

During that year, the threat of German air-raids continued with Zeppelin airships, but even more deadly were the twin-engine Gotha bomber biplanes now attacking London. Biggin Hill was chosen to accommodate one of the Home Defence Squadrons, which would take off to try and engage the enemy on its route into London. The new squadron was No. 141, it arrived on 9th February 1918, but initially it was not fully operational, so aircraft from No. 39 Squadron based at Sutton's Farm, Hornchurch, flew in to cover the gap, as 141 Squadron worked up to become fully ready to take up its role.

The squadron was made up of three Flights A, B and C. A Flight had three Sopwith Dolphin and five Bristol fighters, B Flight were equipped with Bristol F2B fighters and C Flight with BE12s. It was initially planned that the whole squadron was to be equipped with the Sopwith Dolphin, but these were unsuitable for night flying and suffered regular engine breakdowns.

Success for Biggin Hill against the enemy, came on the night of 19th/20th May 1918, when at around 12.30am, Lieutenants Edward Turner and Henry Barwise observed from their Bristol RE8 fighter at 12,000 feet and just a few miles from Biggin Hill, a single Gotha bomber flying above them. They went into the attack and poured rounds of tracer bullets into the enemy, but could see little effect. The German aircraft was lost from sight briefly, before they sighted it again rapidly losing altitude. The German was then attacked by another British fighter, a Sopwith Camel of No. 143 Squadron flown by Major Frederick Sowrey. The Gotha finally crash landed at Frinsted in Kent, two of the crew killed, while the third, the air-gunner survived with only a broken arm.

There was speculation as to who had delivered the final blow to bring down the Gotha, but when the German gunner, Unteroffizier Hermann Tasche was questioned in hospital, he told his interviewer that the RE8 had dealt the fatal damage. As the news arrived at Biggin Hill, the men of No. 141 celebrated with cheers and a great many drinks. This was the first victory for the squadron and Biggin Hill. Both men were later awarded the Distinguished Flying Cross and the German Cross was cut from one of the Gotha's wings and was hung as a trophy in the squadrons' mess.

During March 1918, work had begun on construction of permanent buildings such as barrack blocks, officers' mess, wireless research and concrete hangar for the large amount of service personnel that worked at the airfield. Conditions were not ideal while the building work continued throughout the winter of 1918/1919, many personnel having to live under canvas, without hot water or heating. The South Camp area was finally completed and returned to normality.

That year, the Instrument Design Establishment was set up and established at Biggin Hill, where it carried out various experiments such as, aircraft landings in fog and mist, sonic discs to send out high frequency sound to guide pilots back to base. This unit remained at the base for the next four years before moving to Farnborough.

In 1923, another unit was established within the South Camp at Biggin Hill. This was the Army's Anti-Aircraft School along with the Search-Light Experimental Establishment and Acoustic Section, who moved into the buildings once accommodating the Instrument Design Establishment.

During this period, the only squadron operating from the airfield was No. 56; they had flown in from Hawkinge to Biggin in May 1923 and were mainly tasked with carrying out air exercises in co-operation with the army. A Night Flying Training Flight was also formed in 1923, to train pilots to adapt to flying at night and assist the Army School of Anti-Aircraft Defence for night exercises simulating bomber attacks. The bomber available at this time was the large Vickers Vimy, the same kind of aircraft that the two RAF pioneers John Alcock and Arthur Brown had used to fly the first non-stop flight across the Atlantic from Newfoundland and crash-landing in a bog in County Galway, Ireland on 15th June 1919.

This gigantean measured 43-feet in length and had a wingspan of 68-feet and Biggin Hill's flightpath was small, so getting the heavy lumbering Vimy bombers airborne was a feat in itself.

These night-time exercises carried on regularly for several months and the local population suffered many sleepless nights, so much so that the Royal Air Force was condemned and ridiculed for its lack of thought towards the locals living near to the aerodrome, especially in the villages of Downe and Cudham.

During 1924, 56 Squadron was re-equipped with the latest RAF fighter biplane, the Gloster Grebe. The Grebe was designed by Henry Folland and had entered service with the RAF in October 1923. It had a maximum speed of 152 mph powered its Armstrong Siddeley Jaguar IV 14-cylinder air-cooled engine which gave 400 horse-power; it could fly to a height of 23,000 feet.

Tragedy was to strike during the winter of 1924, when while conducting an air-defence exercise for a film unit, which had been invited by the Air Ministry to record a sequence of flying that entailed No. 56 Squadron re-enacting a dogfight with a Vimy bomber. The filming was to be done by another Vickers Vimy following in close support. As the first bomber approached, 56 Squadron were scrambled to intercept and soon their Gloster Grebes were taking turns to dive down and attack.

The crew in the leading Vimy, had been asked to simulate the shooting down of their aircraft by lighting flares as it lost height over the village of Cudham. The cameraman in the following aircraft was still filming the sequence, when the first aircraft suddenly crashed into the ground, into a wooded area before coming to a sudden halt with black smoke billowing from the engines. The pilot having misjudged his height had lost control of his aircraft; both crewmen were killed.

Following the parliamentary report into the expansion of the Royal Air Force in 1923, Biggin Hill was one of a number of aerodromes that was chosen to be enlarged. No. 56 Squadron left Biggin Hill in October 1927 and moved to their new base at RAF North Weald.

Twenty-nine extra acres of land was purchased and construction began in 1927 to enlarge the North Camp, which still had old wooden accommodation huts left over from the Great War. The building of a new officers' mess, barrack blocks, cook house and married quarters were all completed by September 1932; when the aerodrome was re-opened under the command of Wing Commander G.B. Dacre DSO, who under his responsibilities was also the Anti-Aircraft Co-Operation Unit, but he was replaced in February 1933 by Wing Commander E.O Grenfell MC, DFC, AFC.

Two new squadrons took up residence that September; No. 32 Squadron arrived on 21st with Bristol Bulldogs commanded by Squadron Leader Baker and No. 23 flying Bulldogs, Hawker Harts and Demons; both had been previously based at RAF Kenley. 32 Squadron received a new commanding officer in December that year, when Squadron Leader D.L. Blackford replaced Baker

During the next few years the squadrons participated in the annual Hendon Air Pageant and the Empire Air Day displays, when the aerodrome would open its gates to the public and give aerobatic displays and feature the latest aircraft designs coming online within the RAF.

By 1936, alarm bells were sounding across Europe in regards to the German armaments expansion, ordered by the new German Chancellor Adolf Hitler, including the building of a new air force, which had been banned by the Versailles Treaty after the end of the First World War.

That year, Biggin Hill was introduced into the newly organised Home Defence Force of Fighter Command under its new commander Air Chief Marshal Sir Hugh Dowding as part of No. 11 Group, which would protect any act of aggression over the south-east of England.

It was Dowding who was instrumental in gaining the funding from the government in the newly invented aircraft detecting system known as RDF (Radio Direction Finding) which was the brainchild of scientist Robert Watson-Watt. Later known as Radar, this was the first system that could pick up a signal from a flying aircraft and relay the information back to give its course and height. The building of RDF aerial towers soon covered an area along the east coast covering from the Wash and down to the Channel and south-east.

One new arrival to take up his first squadron posting was Peter Malam Brothers from Prestwich in Lancashire. He had already obtained a private flying licence at the age of sixteen, before entering into the RAF on a short service commission in January 1936. On his arrival to join No. 32 Squadron as a brand new pilot officer, he was taken to meet the commanding officer and then to the officers' mess to be shown where his room was. His first impressions of the aerodrome during his first weeks there were:

> It was a very nice airfield and the station had purpose built barrack blocks with its own officers' and non-commissioned officers' messes. The food was excellent and consisted of at least four courses. We had to wear our mess uniforms and black ties and were waited upon by stewards, but this was only on guest nights which took place on Thursdays. The daily routine was you had to be on parade by 8.00 am for hoisting of the RAF ensign and then an inspection would take place by the station commander before you then went off down to your hangar and met your flight commander, who would give you your instructions for the morning. You might fly that day; it all depended on the weather conditions.

At Biggin, home defence exercises were undertaken, with No. 32 Squadron practising the new science in conjunction with the newly built operations room, whose controllers would practice the art of sending information to the pilots, giving them various courses and heights to fly to intercept a possible enemy threat.

A new squadron was formed at the aerodrome on 22nd March 1937, when a number of pilots were taken from 'B' Flight of No. 32 Squadron and named as No. 79 Squadron; 'B' Flight commanded by Squadron Leader A.W.B. McDonald came as a complete unit with their own ground crew and aircraft and were changed to 'A' Flight, while other pilots and personnel were posted in to make up a new 'B' Flight. The new squadron was equipped with fourteen Gloster Gauntlet Mk II biplanes which were fitted with the Bristol Mercury VI radial air-cooled engine, flown in from the Storage Unit, Waddington, Lincolnshire. They would be known later as No. 79 'Madras Presidency' Squadron.

The squadron participated in a large Wing formation at the Empire Air Display at the aerodrome on 24th May and the standard set was considered to be exceptionally high

Both squadrons were now equipped with the Gloster Gauntlet fighter biplane during this period. By 1938, the aerodrome had undergone further alterations in security with the C-Type Belfast hangars being repainted with a camouflage scheme, this was done hopefully to confuse the German Lufthansa Airline pilots who were at that time secretly photographing British airfields for German intelligence.

On 11th August 1938, Biggin Hill received its first RAF single low-wing monoplane, when a Miles Magister two-seat trainer touched down. This aircraft was used to familiarise the pilots, who were in a few weeks to receive the new Hawker Hurricane fighter, which was coming online to Fighter Command Squadrons.

As German aggression continued following Hitler's call for the annexation of the borders, parts of Czechoslovakia, whose inhabitants were mainly German speaking people in an area known as the 'Sudetenland;' the two main powers of France and Britain called for a meeting to resolve the situation and arranged for a meeting near Munich with Herr Hitler in September 1938. The State of Czechoslovakia was not even invited to the conference and felt betrayed by its two Allies.

At Biggin Hill, as with other aerodromes around the country, they were brought to a 'state of readiness' for war, should the political leaders fail to find a solution to the ongoing crisis. The code word for the operation was titled 'Diablo.'

With war possibly looming, the aerodrome undertook various changes, such as, camouflaging of buildings and disguising the flightpaths using bitumen tar, hopefully to simulate hedgerows, if viewed from the air by an enemy aircraft. Aeroplanes were quickly painted by the ground crews with some pilots helping out, covering their previously silver finish with green and dark brown camouflage. Some buildings were protected with sandbag reinforcements and blast pens were constructed at various aircraft dispersal points around the perimeter track of the aerodrome. Army anti-aircraft units moved in and set up their defences to repel any attacks should war be declared.

One pilot who arrived at Biggin Hill was Pilot Officer Douglas Hamilton Grice; he hailed from Wallasey, Cheshire and before entering into the RAF had served in the 'Artists Rifles' of the Territorial Army. He was granted a short service commission in the Royal Air Force in December 1937 and after completing his flying training at No. 5 Flying Training

School at Sealand was posted to join No. 32 Squadron on September 17th 1938. Known by his nickname of 'Grubby' he remembers his early days:

> Our first commander in the squadron was a chap named 'Reggie' Pyne who I think had been a First World War pilot; the station commander was Wing Commander 'Fiery' Lock. I was put into A Flight and I remember that all the members were given nicknames. They were commanded by a chap named Pat Connelly who was sadly killed out in the Middle East in 1941, he was known as the 'Bulldog' and the reason for that was quite apparent if you had seen him. His No. 2 was Michael Crossley, he was 'Red Knight' he was a debonair Old Estonian with a very great presence; he looked like a knight for a start.
>
> There was another delightful chap named John Milner, who never took life very seriously, he was a great artist and a marvellous golfer and smoked like a chimney, mostly Camel cigarettes, but was a sort of dreamy individual, he was nicknamed 'Millie the Moucher' after one of the cartoon characters in the Popeye comics.
>
> We had two other pilots, Proctor and White, Proctor was called 'Hector' and Sergeant White had to be 'Chalky.' I had already acquired a nickname by then and I was always known as 'Grubby' and this arose initially on my very first day at elementary flying training school. I was meeting some of the new chaps I'd never met before in my life and we were introducing ourselves to one another. I was then introduced to somebody named 'Folkes' as Douglas Grice. He looked at me and took my hands and off the top of his head he said 'Grice, Grice 'Grubby' Grice. And from that day onwards I have been known as 'Grubby.'

On 24th September, the crisis in Europe worsened, when Hitler issued the 'Godesburg Memorandum,' which demanded that Czechoslovakia concede the Sudetenland to Germany, no later than 28th September. A deal was finally reached at 1.30 am on 30th September 1938, when

Neville Chamberlain, Edouard Daladier, Benito Mussolini and Adolf Hilter signed the Munich Agreement.

The plan, which gave Germany the right to occupy the Sudetenland, but stated that Germany could not pursue any further advances into Czechoslovakia, was drawn up by Mussolini, although in truth it was produced by the German Foreign Office. The news of the agreement was relayed to the Czech Government, who were told that they would either have to stand against Germany alone or accept the deal put forward, which they did. Upon his return that day to Heston aerodrome, Neville Chamberlain stepped from the aeroplane and greeted the newspaper reporters and film crews, brandishing a copy of the Anglo-German document, declaring 'Peace in our time.'

By the 17th October, No. 32 Squadron had been fully equipped with the new Hawker Hurricane Mk1 eight gun mono-plane receiving 14 aircraft in total. Their radio call-sign was to be 'Jacko.'

On 15th November 1938, Biggin Hill received a new station commander, when Wing Commander Richard Grice took over from Wing Commander Lock. Grice had distinguished himself during the First World War, becoming an ace whilst flying over the Western Front with No. 8 Squadron and was awarded the Distinguished Flying Cross. He was a tall, slim figure and gave the impression of a thoughtful and fair person. During his time at Biggin Hill, he would become the most respected of commanding officers by all the personnel both pilots, ground crews and WAAFs.

# Chapter 2
# 1939
# The Outbreak of War

At the start of 1939, the main layout of the aerodrome's landing paths consisted of an east to west path of 710 yards with a larger south-west to north-west area of 2,000 yards and also from north to south of 1,666 yards with a further area from north-east to south-west of 1,333 yards. Later that autumn a further runway would be laid measuring 1,600 by 50 yards.

No. 79 Squadron suffered the loss of one of their Hurricane aircraft L1782 on 27th February, whilst undertaking air exercises, when Rhodesian born Pilot Officer Frederick John Lawrence Duus was overcome by fumes from the Rolls Royce engine which filled the cockpit and he had no option but to vacate the aircraft at a height of 2,000 feet, one mile north of Bekesbourne, Kent and take to his parachute. He was able to land safely at Littlebourne.

On 25th April 1939, No. 3 Squadron based at RAF Kenley started their move to go to Biggin Hill to convert from their Gloster Gladiators back to Hawker Hurricane fighters and by 1st May, ground crew personnel had taken over the South Camp. The next day, Squadron Leader Chapman arrived with the remainder of the squadron and four Hurricane aircraft were ferried into the airfield for their use. By the 15th May, the squadron had 10 Hurricanes and a Fairey Battle aircraft.

The squadron suffered two unfortunate accidents to pilots within the space of two-days, when on 29th May, Acting Flight Lieutenant L. M. Gaunce collided with a motor car whilst riding his motorcycle outside the South Camp Guard Room, and he was taken to Uxbridge Hospital for treatment. The following day, a Hurricane aircraft, L1938 suffered engine failure as its pilot; Pilot Officer Hallifax prepared to come into land. He spun into a cornfield and crashed, luckily he only suffered from slight concussion, but was sent to hospital, where he remained for a week before being sent on sick leave. On his return he took over as squadron adjutant.

One of the serving officers of No. 3 Squadron during this time was Pilot Officer Hedley Neville Fowler; his father was a Paymaster Commander in the Royal Navy and was the great grandson of Sir Henry Ayers, of South Australia whom Ayers Rock had been named after. Born in London in 1916 and educated at Rugby School, the family moved between England and Australia during the 1920s and 30s. Fowler enlisted in the Royal Australian Air Force in 1936, before transferring to the Royal Air Force and was granted a short service commission in February 1937. He was posted to No. 3 Squadron on 22nd May 1937 and remained with them until October 1939, when he was posted to 615 Squadron; who were then sent to France in November that year as part of the Air Component of the Allied Expeditionary Force.

When the squadron was heavily involved in action from 10th May 1940 following the German invasion in Holland, Belgium and France; Fowler claimed his first victory and that of the squadron on 12th May, against an Me109. He claimed two more of the enemy before being shot down himself on 14th May. He baled-out and landed in the Ardennes Forest safely, where he met some French soldiers who were in retreat. However, the following day, he was captured along with his French comrades. He was sent to numerous prison camps before ending up at the infamous Colditz Castle in December 1941.

Here he was involved with many unsuccessful escape attempts, and then on the 9th September 1942, with a Dutch officer, Lieutenant Damien Joan van Doormick, they successful escaped the castle and crossed into Switzerland on 13th September, where they were taken to the British Embassy at Bern. He finally arrived back in Britain in March 1943

Fowler was awarded the Military Cross for his successful escape. He was promoted to squadron leader and was posted to the Armament Test Squadron at Boscombe Down to act as a test pilot. Sadly, he was to lose his life test flying a Hawker Typhoon fighter aircraft on 26th March

1944. He was 27 years old.

During the month of April, the squadrons at Biggin prepared for what was to be the last Empire Air Day. Each RAF airfield held an open day for the public, and the squadrons at Biggin rehearsed for the show between the 16th/19th May. A record crowd of 21,300 attended the event on 20th May. The flying programme started at 2.00 pm with an individual aerobatic display by a Gloster Gauntlet, whose pilot was able to communicate with the public by loudspeakers situated around the aerodrome explaining the various manoeuvres he was about to undertake. This was followed by a demonstration of gliding; then at 2.40 pm six Hurricanes took off rapidly to intercept a formation of three Blenheims.

A physical training display was carried out by No. 21 (Lewisham) Air Defence Cadet Corps, which brought much applause. The A.R.P Borough of Beckenham also undertook a demonstration showing how to react to the threat of an air-raid and aid to casualties. At 4.00 pm there was a mass flight over the aerodrome by thirty Avro Ansons. The day's finale came at 6.00 pm, when all the aircraft that had been exhibited in the aircraft park took off and flew past in succession. These included a Fairey Battle, Airspeed Oxford, Gloster Gladiator, North American Harvard, Westland Lysander and a Short Scion.

On 9th June, the aerodrome was visited by the Secretary of State for Air, Sir Kingsley Wood, accompanied by Leslie Hore-Belisha, the Secretary of State for War. During their stay, they were photographed with RAF Officers and a number of aircraft some of which they boarded. They also observed trials of an unnamed prototype fighter aircraft.

The aerodrome suffered the loss of a pilot on Tuesday 20th June 1939, when Flight Sergeant Leonard Frank Davis, a 26 year old Volunteer Reserve airman attached to No.79 Squadron was killed, when his Hawker Hurricane L1593 crashed on Ditchling Common, not far from Burgess Hill, Sussex, during a severe thunderstorm shortly before 3.00 pm. The accident was witnessed by many people on the ground, their attention being attracted by a strange whistling noise, when they saw an aircraft appear from heavy cloud and dive almost vertically at a terrific speed. As the machine hurtled to destruction, a parachute fluttered from the cockpit dragging the pilot with it.

The tremendous strain caused the harness to snap and the pilot fell like a stone to his death. Members of the public rushed to the spot and found the unfortunate pilot lying nearby amongst the twisted metalwork of the plane, which had buried itself into the ground. Wreckage was scattered over an area of 200-yards. The police were quickly on the scene and the body of Flight Sergeant Davis was taken to the Burgess Hill mortuary.

The crater around which a number of live belts of ammunition was found was fenced off and guarded throughout the night by aircraftsmen, who on the following day retrieved as much of the aircraft as possible.

Giving evidence at the inquiry that followed, Flight Lieutenant Claude Roberts of 79 Squadron said that Davis had been attached to the squadron since February, and had 62-hours of flying time on Hurricane fighters. Roberts stated that Davis was entirely on his own and was in no way connected with any other machine during the flight. On visiting the crash-site, the whole of the engine was completely buried and it was impossible to say whether anything went wrong with the machine.

He had examined the parachute, which was badly torn and the harness was broken, but no attempt had been made by the pilot to use it. The D-ring which released the parachute had not been pulled. It would have been very difficult for the pilot to have got out of an aircraft in a vertical dive. As the aircraft was seen to disappear into dark cloud, and when it reappeared diving almost vertically, it was summarised that Sgt Davis had not settled down to the instruments and he had pushed his aircraft down to get below cloud-level, rather than fly through it. In doing so, he misjudged his height and was unable to pull out.

During the summing up, the coroner said that the pilot had a fair amount of experience, but the aircraft was so hopelessly broken up, that it was impossible to say what caused it to fail. The jury returned a verdict of accidental death on Flight Sergeant Davis caused through falling with damaged parachute.

No. 79 Squadron received notice on the 3rd July, that they had been selected as one of five squadrons to represent the Royal Air Force in Paris, during the celebrations for the 150th Anniversary of the 'Storming of the Bastille. On 10th, the squadron consisting of 11 aircraft took off from Biggin Hill led by Squadron Leader C.C. McMullen and headed for Le Bourget; their ground personnel travelled to Paris by rail and boat. For the following two days nine of the Hurricane aircraft participated in rehearsals for the display and was also inspected by the French Air Minister. On 14th, they flew in the mass flight over the Arc de Triomphe and along the Champs Elysees before returning home to Biggin, after re-fuelling at Le Bourget.

On 9th July, 32 Squadron suffered the loss of Hawker Hurricane L1661 whilst over the Kent coast, its pilot Patrick Edward Geoffrey Connolly from Tunbridge Wells had to bale-out following mechanical failure; the aircraft plunged into the ground south of Herne Bay, Kent. Connolly would later transfer to Bomber Command and reach the rank of wing commander before being killed in action flying Lancaster LL837 with No. 550 Squadron on 15th July 1944

Tragedy was to strike No. 32 Squadron during the evening of 11th August. Whilst undertaking a 'Black–Out' exercise, Pilot Officer Harold Stewart Olding aged 19 was killed when his Hurricane L1567 crashed into a hillside at Tatsfield, Surrey, two-miles from the airfield at 12.15 am. The son of Harold John Olding, of Wellington Road, Enfield, North London; he had attended the Ponders End Technical Institute, where he studied many phases of engineering. While there, he helped with the editing of the school magazine and contributed flying stories to it. He took up flying at the Herts and Essex Flying Club at Broxbourne, before being accepted into the Royal Air Force at 18. Following a course at Hamble, near Southampton, he was sent to various RAF Stations before arriving at Biggin Hill

Robert Jackson, the station engineer at Biggin Hill, stated that shortly after midnight, he saw an illumination in the south followed by the sound of an engine faltering and then a dull thud. From previous experience, he knew what had happened and a fire tender was immediately despatched from the airfield. A second aircraft was ordered to take-off and fire off flares to guide the tender and ambulance to the crash-site.

The second aircraft, Hurricane L1662, which was being flown by Flying Officer Arthur Robin Buchanan-Wollaston also crashed soon after, killing its pilot. Buchanan-Wollaston aged 26 was the only son of Vice-Admiral H.A. Buchanan-Wollaston C.M.G. of Tavistock, Devon. The inquest was held at RAF Biggin Hill, conducted by Mr W.A. Thomson, Deputy Coroner for West Kent and was assisted by a jury, the Foreman being Councillor J.R. Guthrie.

During the proceedings the following eye-witness statements were given. Squadron Leader Thomas Bain Prickman said 'Olding was a fully qualified pilot and had 150-hours flying experience. He had one previous accident, due to engine trouble.'

Edward Warren, an air-raid patrol warden gave evidence and said he was in St. John's Road, Tatsfeld at 12.15 am and heard the sound of the aircraft. He saw a bright light which lit up the area. The light was near the ground and he thought that it was an indication bomb, probably dropped by a plane in connection with the 'black-out.' He then heard an engine stop and then the sound of a crash. He made his way to the crash by following the wreckage and found a body near the aircraft. There was considerable fog in patches at the time of the crash, although at midnight it was perfectly clear.

Flying Officer James St. Clair Polson, the medical officer at Biggin Hill who had been on duty that night gave evidence and stated, 'Olding had been with the squadron since January 10th 1939.' Continuing, Polson said that he had heard the first crash at 12.15 and went out with the ambulance. Twenty minutes later, he found the aircraft and Olding lying beside the Hurricane in a field known as The Park. The body was only laying two-yards from the aircraft. Death was due to a fracture of the base of the skull. There were signs that the machine had travelled some distance along the ground before it came to rest.

Polson then related information regarding the second fatal incident. While he was in attendance on the first crash at 12.40 am, he heard the second crash at Luxted Hall Farm, Tatsfield. When he reached the spot at 1.10 am, he found the deceased badly mutilated. The wrecked aircraft was on one side of the hedge and the pilot had evidently been thrown over the hedge and through a coppice of trees.

Squadron Leader Prickman stated that Buchanan-Wollaston had been at the station since September 1937 and was acting flight commander that evening. After the first crash, he had been instructed to fly over the scene and drop a flare to enable the ambulance to locate it. Prickman continued 'I think he showed error of judgement when meeting the low cloud, not climbing above them instead of trying to get underneath them. He evidently lost his bearings and in an endeavour to turn back to the aerodrome struck the ground.'

The verdict of the inquest stated that both pilots must have been affected by adverse weather conditions at low level and was recorded as 'accidental death.'

On 15th August, both pilots were given a joint funeral at Cudham Parish Church. Shortly before 11.am, the coffins were taken from the camp hospital and to a slow march, borne to the tender, where they were covered with the Union Jack and beautiful flowers and wreaths. The cortege, which included the whole of the personnel of No. 32 Squadron, made its way to the church and was led by Wing Commander Grice, the station commander. Special police were on duty and members of the A.R.P at Cudham, helped to line the path to the church. The service was conducted by the Reverend W. Hope-Gill. Both airmen were then laid to rest within the church cemetery.

No. 3 Squadron carried out its first night-flying training on 29th August; all landed safely following the flight accept for Sergeant Butterick who crashed on landing in Hurricane L1928 which was badly damaged, fortunately the pilot was unhurt.

The squadron received orders the following day to move to their new base at Croydon, which they did on the morning of 2nd September1939, taking over the two southernmost hangars previously used by 'Sabena,' K.L.M and Air France Air Lines.

On that same day, another squadron flew in to Biggin Hill to take up operations, this was No. 601 Auxiliary Squadron (County of London) also nicknamed the 'Millionaires' due to the fact that most of their pilots had come from well to do families in society. The aircraft they were using during this period was the short-nosed Bristol Blenheim Mk1F, a twin-engine light-bomber.

Within their ranks were a number of pilots who during the war, would become outstanding fighter aces and leaders; there was Pilot Officer John William Maxwell Aitkin, the son of newspaper tycoon, Lord Beaverbrook; Flying Officer Archibald Hope the son of 17th Baronet of Craighall, he finished the war as a group captain and was successful in the aviation business being awarded an OBE.

There was Flight Lieutenant Roger Bushell who was a pre-war accomplished winter skier and barrister, who later led the escape from Stalag Luft III (The Great Escape) in March 1944. He was one of seventy-six escapees, and one of fifty who were later recaptured by the Germans and murdered by the Gestapo under Hitler's orders.

Another was American born Whitney Willard Straight, the son of New York Mayor and oriental expert Willard Straight. Educated in England at Darlington Hall and then Trinity College, Cambridge, he learnt to fly and owned his own aeroplane and was also an excellent racing car driver. He became a British citizen in 1935; he entered business and formed his own company 'Straight Corporation,' an airline passenger carrier which was extremely successful before the outbreak of war. Jack Cladburn served as an armourer with 601 Squadron and remembers his time with them:

> I joined No. 601 Auxiliary Squadron firstly at Hendon. They were named the 'Millionaires' Squadron and had switched over to Bristol Blenheims when I arrived; we were then posted to Biggin Hill. We used to get all our food in the NAAFI and we had comfortable accommodation in huts. The Blenheim was being converted to a twin-engine fighter at this time, which meant we took out the bomb racks in the bomb bay and we fitted in a conversion unit of four 303 inch browning machine guns. This was fitted and bolted into the bomb bay and this converted the aircraft to a five gun

aircraft. One of the pilots I remember was Lord Beaverbrook's son, Max Aitkin and also Whitney Straight the racing driver was another. They seemed OK and used to mix in with us, although they all used to pull up in chauffeur driven cars. In fact while I was there I went up to the auxiliary warrant officer and he asked me what rank was I and I replied 'AC2,' he replied 'we don't have AC2s in this squadron,' the next time he came around, he had promoted me to AC1. After that I was again promoted to Leading Aircraftsman, so I did fairly well.

It is recorded that soon after their arrival at the aerodrome, they were challenged by members of No. 32 Squadron to a Polo game using motorcycles. No. 32 Squadron arrived for the game with various machines, whilst 601 were equipped with more or less brand new Brough SS100 and SS80 Superiors. 601 totally outrode their opposition and won the game.

As news arrived on Friday 1st September, that the German armed forces had crossed the border into Poland, Britain and France were now on the point of war. Both countries had given their word that any aggression against the Poles would lead to conflict against Hitler's Nazi Germany.

At Biggin Hill that day, airmen's families who lived in the married quarters were given two hours to prepare to leave. Six months earlier plans had been arranged by the Air Ministry to evacuate non–service personnel to main London railway stations from where they would travel to pre-arranged accommodation in various parts of England. The rest of the aerodrome was put on imminent war footing.

On the morning of Sunday 3rd September 1939 at 11.10 am, wireless sets around Britain gave out Prime Minister Neville Chamberlain's news that Great Britain was now at war with Germany, following the invasion of Poland by Nazi forces two-days earlier and that Adolf Hitler had ignored the French and British ultimatum to withdraw.

At Biggin Hill the news was not unexpected and many servicemen and women, although feeling the tension of the moment, soon went about their duties with the realisation of what may lie ahead. Soon after Chamberlain's speech, the sound could be heard of wailing air-raid sirens and the immediate fear of the local population; that waves of German bombers would suddenly appear and begin dropping their bombs, causing death and destruction, as they made their way for the shelters. Of course this was totally not possible, as no German fighter or bomber aircraft had the range or fuel capacity to reach Britain at this period without re-fuelling.

Douglas Grice of 32 Squadron remembers the morning of the outbreak of war:

> On September 3rd 1939, I seem to remember listing to the wireless and to the announcement that we were at war with Germany, and we all gave a loud cheer that at long last we would earn our keep, it was really quite exhilarating. We did not quite know what was to come, but we were all fully trained as well as we could have been.

However, No. 32 Squadron who were out on dispersal received orders when their mobile telephone rang and gave them instructions for 'Blue' Section to immediately get airborne and patrol the Gravesend area, as an unidentified aircraft had been picked up by RDF flying up the Channel. Unbeknown to 'Blue' Section, it transpired that the unknown aircraft was a French transport and had touched down safely at Croydon Airport.

More anxious moments occurred during that same day, when in the afternoon the Maidstone Searchlight Control reported that Army sound detectors had picked up aircraft in the vicinity. At Biggin, 601 Squadron was ordered to take-off and investigate, while on the ground the anti-aircraft defences had been brought to action. The alert turned out to be a complete fiasco, when it was discovered that the sensitive Mk VIII sound detectors had not picked up an aircraft engine at all, but the noise made by a refrigerator's electric motor, the door of the room in which it was placed, had been left open.

Biggin Hill lost its first pilot following the outbreak of war on 11th

September 1939, when Flight Lieutenant Richard Reynolds who commanded 'A' Flight of No. 79 Squadron, whilst undertaking a night-flying practice crashed his Hurricane aircraft into trees at Holt Wood, Chelsham, two and half miles south-west of the aerodrome and was killed instantly. He was buried at the local churchyard at Cudham. At this time the squadron's radio call-sign was 'Pansy.'

Within days, four Hurricane squadrons consisting of No's 1, 73, 85 and 87 were on their way to bases situated in Northern France as part of the Advanced Air Striking Force which also consisted of Bristol Blenheim and Fairey Battle light bomber squadrons in support of the British Expeditionary Force army who were being sent to reinforce the French.

During the first few weeks, there was little activity in the air or on the ground, as France and Britain prepared for Hitler's next move. What was he up to, after easily defeating the Polish army and air force? Occasionally, the RAF would sight German reconnaissance aircraft intruding into French airspace along the border, but there was very little in the way of combat; perhaps the odd skirmish.

This period of waiting, began to make the civilian population wonder if there really was a war going on and therefore it was labelled the 'Phoney War'.

The squadrons remained on alert throughout the rest of September, but very little air activity was accomplished. Only on the 17th September, did an incident occur, when a pilot was ordered to take-off and shot down a Barrage balloon that had come adrift from its moorings and was becoming a hazard? The pilot intercepted the drifting balloon at a height of 25,000 feet, but during his climb, the pilot had forgotten to ensure his oxygen was turned on before taking off. As a result, he passed out, but fortunately came to after his aircraft had fallen to 10,000 feet. He returned to the aerodrome and landed safely. It was later understood that he punctured the balloon and that some of his bullets dislodged tiles on a house roof at Esher.

The 32 Squadron operations book gives an insight to what was happening at the aerodrome during that first month of war:

Since the outbreak of war, No. 32 Squadron has been operating from a dispersal point on the east side of the aerodrome. A temporary camp of tents has been erected there to enable the pilots and crews to sleep near their machines.
Work is progressing rapidly on the aerodrome with the construction of concrete runways and taxying tracks. A new dispersal point on the south side of the aerodrome was allotted to 32 Squadron during the month, and plans for the semi-dispersal point have been made out by Squadron Leader T.B. Prickman. Three wooden huts (50 feet x 18 feet) are being constructed and are almost completed.
During the last fortnight of the month, both A and B Flights have been engaged in training their new pilots. This is progressing well. During the month, the squadron carried out night flying, squadron formation, squadron attacks as well as individual training.

The following month of October, the squadrons at the aerodrome continued with many luckless flights, having been sent up to investigate unidentified aircraft picked up by RDF, titled as X-Raids; many turning out to be friendly aircraft on training flights or coming back from France. The weather that month was also very unsettled with much rain; so some days flying was not possible. Douglas Grice remembers the frustration felt by the pilots during this period caused by the pointless patrols being sent off from Biggin Hill to investigate the false alarms, caused them to compose the following comical verse:

The Plots that appear on the Screen, tra la,
have nothing to do with the Hun.
The AOC's having a dream, tra la
And won't send us off in a stream, tra la,
to fight the Hun in the sun.
And that's what I mean when I say and I scream.
Oh bother the plots that appear on the screen!

On 30th October, 32 Squadron bade farewell to their squadron commander Tom Prickman who was given command of RAF Stradishall and was promoted to the rank of wing commander. The squadrons' new leader was Squadron Leader Robert Alexander Chignall, who was already well known to many of the pilots, having served there since July 1938 at the aerodromes Sector Headquarters.

The first enemy aircraft destroyed by a Biggin Hill squadron was claimed on 21st November, when two Hurricanes flown by Flying Officer 'Jimmy' Davies, an American and Flight Sergeant Brown took off from their forward base at Manston and were given instructions to patrol over Hawkinge at 10.00 am. Once airborne they headed along the south coast and began to patrol. After only 20-minutes they were then asked to check out an unidentified plot over Dover. This turned out to be an Avro Anson aircraft of Coastal Command. Finally after several more minutes, they received a new heading at 10.50 am and were given a new course by the controller.

Out over the Channel, they sighted a single Dornier 17Z bomber on a weather reconnaissance mission. The two pilots who were 3,000 feet above the German dived into the attack and fired off their machine guns at a range of 600 yards. After three independent attacks, the Dornier began to stream black smoke from one of its engines and pieces of airframe began to fall away. No return fire was observed from the bombers rear-gunner, probably due to the German pilots evasive manoeuvring. The Dornier slowly rolled over and spun down through the clouds before plunging into the sea and exploding. This was witnessed by both pilots.

No. 601 Squadron had the distinction of becoming the first squadron based at Biggin Hill during the war, to take the fight to the enemy, when they took off on 28th November 1939, in company with No. 25 Squadron also flying Blenheims, to undertake a raid against the Luftwaffe seaplane base at Borkum Island, part of the Frisian Islands, of Lower Saxony, north-western Germany.

The previous day, three aircraft of 'A' Flight L8701, L5617 and L6722, along with three from 'B' Flight, L6680, L6720 and L6605 took off from Biggin Hill and flew to RAF Northolt at 2.55 pm. On arrival, the pilots received orders to participate in the projected raid scheduled for the following day. The remaining aircrew, wireless personnel and armourers arrived at Northolt shortly afterwards, and spent the entire night equipping the aircraft for the operation; this was completed by 10.30 am the next morning.

The Blenheims took off in company with six aircraft of 25 Squadron at 11.30 am and flew to Bircham Newton, taking off again for the raid at 2.15 pm, flying in four sections led by Squadron Leader J. R. Hallings-Potts of No. 25 Squadron with Flight Lieutenant M.F. Peacock leading the second section and Flying Officer Aitkin, the fourth.

Flying low over the North Sea at only a few hundred feet, they came in over the German base undetected at 3.30 pm; the British caught the Germans unaware and strafed the seaplanes at their moorings or on the ground, as well as the installations. The Blenheims dived down in a wide echelon formation firing de-Wilde tracer ammunition, which caused considerable damage and left several seaplanes badly damaged and burning. The raid was a success and the two squadrons returned home without any casualties, and made landfall at Great Yarmouth at 5.00 pm. It was decided by Hallings-Potts that they would land at Debden and not return to Northolt that evening as intended, 601 flew back to Biggin on 29th, and received much praise for the successful mission.

Those pilots who carried out the raid belonging to 601 Squadron were Flight Lieutenants Thomas Hubbard, and Michael Peacock, who were awarded the Distinguished Flying Cross, Flying Officers Archibald Hope, Carl Davis, William Rhodes-Moorhouse and Max Aitkin.

No. 79 Squadron were given the important task on 4th December of providing air cover, escorting the destroyer HMS *Codrington* across the Channel to the Port of Boulogne carrying King George on his visit to France, to meet with his generals and French counterparts and inspect the troops of both the French and British armies. They were presented with the same task six days later, when the King returned to England. On the return trip at 9.00 am Squadron Leader McMullen, Flight Lieutenant Crossley, Flying Officer Gracie and Pilot Officer Cross provided the cover. As the destroyer entered Dover harbour, the four Hurricane pilots dived down and flew low near to the naval vessel. The King, who was on the bridge at this time, was seen to give a salute as they flew by.

When they arrived back at Biggin, they were immediately ordered to the station commander's office, where Wing Commander Grice in no uncertain terms, told them of their reckless behaviour and endangering not only themselves, but the King. Soon after, a communique arrived by motorcycle despatch rider in which the King had asked Wing Commander Grice to pass on his thanks to the pilots for their escort and the low-flying display they had undertaken on his arrival back in Dover. That evening the station commander bought the pilots a round of drinks as an apology for his dressing down earlier that day.

Throughout the rest of December, the squadrons carried out their monotonous tasks of convoy and X-Raid patrols. As Christmas approached, the aerodrome was visited by the Secretary of State for Air, Sir Arthur Kingsley Wood; where he was invited to the Sergeant's and Officers' Messes. On arrival with Group Captain Grice, he wished everybody a 'Happy Christmas.' Sitting down to dinner, Kingsley Wood and Grice had their meal and drinks served by the senior ranks and non-commissioned officers who also served the junior officers and men in attendance. During the festivities a BBC Radio Broadcasting crew arrived at the station and recorded the celebrations being held. It was later broadcast over the airwaves as 'Christmas Day at a Fighter Squadron.' So ended a year that saw Europe once again plunged into conflict with Germany.

# Chapter 3
# 1940
## France & Dunkirk

At the start of January 1940, all three of Biggin Hill's squadrons were moved off the aerodrome as construction gangs came in to build extra deep air-raid shelters and an extra short runway. No. 32 Squadron was packed off to Gravesend, where they set up at the small flying club; 79 Squadron went down to Manston and 601 to Tangmere in Sussex.

During this period, Britain saw one of the severest winters on record and heavy snow made it impossible for aircraft to fly. Only at Gravesend did 32 Squadron manage to get airborne because the biting wind coming in across the Thames Estuary never allowed the snow to settle. The ground personnel were put to work with shovels and brooms to clear some of the snow off the runways and the aircraft.

A new young fresh-faced pilot arrived to take up his first posting to No. 32 Squadron on 5th February; this man was Pilot Officer Donald William Alfred Stones aged 19. Stones came from Norwich and had been educated at Ipswich Grammar School. He had been destined pre-war to enter into the insurance business, but decided to enter into the Royal Air Force and was granted a short service commission in early May 1939. It was with 32 Squadron the following month that he was christened with the nickname of 'Dimsie' which would remain with him throughout the remainder of his service career and his lifetime. The nickname came about when one day while the squadron was detached to Gravesend; he had quickly stuffed into his coat pocket a book, as he rushed to the mess hall for breakfast. The book was titled 'Dimsie goes to school.' His fellow pilots had noticed the title and joked with him about it. From then on he was known as 'Dimsie.'

Donald Stones was a real character and a very good pilot, but on one occasion his zestfulness got him into trouble when visiting the flying club at Brooklands with other 32 Squadron officers. While in the bar, he was asked if he would like a whisky mac from one of the older members, who he took to be of no consequence and ribbed him that he was far too old to fly a Hurricane fighter. Michael Crossley his flight commander beckoned Stones aside and tore him off a strip, calling him a 'bloody' fool! The gentleman, whom Stones had been so condescending to, was in fact the Hawkers Aircraft Chief Test Pilot, George Bulman, who had flown the prototype and many more besides. His stay with 32 Squadron was only brief, as he was posted to serve with Biggin Hill's other squadron, No. 79 on 18th March.

On the afternoon of Sunday 3rd March 1940, a tragic incident occurred in which an RAF aircraft was mistakenly shot down by other friendly aircraft. That afternoon a Lockheed Hudson twin-engine aircraft of the Photographic Development Unit based at Heston was given the task of photographing RAF airfields in the Kent area.

The Hudson N7334 was flying over the Gravesend area at around 7,000 feet and after taking the appropriate photographs was heading back towards London. Suddenly the sky erupted with the sight and sound of anti-aircraft gun-fire, presumably the ground defences had not been informed of a friendly aircraft operating in that area. No. 32 Squadron had been moved to Gravesend aerodrome recently following the alteration and construction of the runways at Biggin Hill; and three Hurricanes were ordered off at 2.30 pm to investigate Raid X27.

The pilots tasked with the interception were Flight Lieutenant Michael Crossley in Hurricane N.2461, and Sergeants' John Proctor N.2462 and John White in N.2460. Climbing up to a height above the Hudson aeroplane, the three Hurricanes moved into a line astern formation and prepared to attack. Later reports state that as the Hurricanes dived down to attack, the crew aboard the Hudson knew what was about to happen and the pilot Flying Officer Sydney Slocum made a steep turn to try and escape; also the crew had fired off two yellow Verey flare lights and signalled with a lamp in an attempt to show that they were friendly.

Sadly this was to no avail and the Hurricanes had begun to pour bullets into the aircraft, which immediately began to catch light and burst into flames. It turned over onto its side and headed earthwards. As the Hudson plunged downwards, a single figure was witnessed falling from the aircraft and then a parachute opened; this was Sergeant John Reid, the co-pilot.

The aircraft broke into three pieces and crashed into open farmland at Happy Valley near Meopham Green, Kent. In his report, Sergeant Reid stated that 'after the Hudson had been attacked and set alight; he had escaped the inferno, but had become entangled by his harness. It was only the explosions from the fuel tanks that had thrown him clear of the wreckage and had blown open his parachute.'

On landing he was helped by a local poultry farmer, Mr P.T. Parnell who had used a gate as a makeshift stretcher to take him to an ambulance and then ferried him to Gravesend Hospital to be treated for burns and other injuries. The bodies of his fellow airmen were found by the police approximately one mile from the wreckage. Those who perished were Flying Officer Slocum aged 29, Wireless Operator-Leading Aircraftsman John Butcher aged 26 and Photographer-Aircraftsman Ronald Mutton aged 20. It was only on their return to Gravesend that the three Hurricane pilots learnt later of their terrible mistake.

No. 32 Squadron suffered the loss of Flying Officer Lancelot Gordon Bowler aged 22-years on a flight over the Channel on 23rd March. He along with Sergeant Duckenfield had been tasked to undertake a convoy patrol. Bowler in Hurricane N2531 with Duckenfield flying N2582 took off at 12.25 pm and headed towards the Folkestone area. When they were about five miles south of Folkestone and two miles out to sea at a height of 1,500 feet, they ran into thick cloud. Bowler continued into the cloud and after about three minutes turned west. Sergeant Duckenfield broke away as he saw that Bowler was in difficulties. From that moment at 12.40 pm, nothing more was heard or seen of Flying Officer Bowler. It is likely that he lost control and dived into the sea; he was reported as missing. No trace of him was ever found and he is remembered on the Runnymede Memorial, Panel 5. He was Biggin Hill's second casualty of the war.

79 Squadron also lost Sergeant Bernard Spencer, when he was killed in a flying accident on 26th April in Hurricane L1709, when it spun into the ground, crashing at Ley House Farm, and north-east of Three Bridges in Sussex. Spencer a native of Dursley in Gloucestershire had joined the RAF in 1930 as an aircraft apprentice and had trained at Halton in Buckinghamshire. After, he became one of the most successful entrants; he entered for air training in August 1938 and on completion of his course was found to be an exceptional, reliable and competent pilot at the time of his death

Of the new personnel who arrived at the aerodrome during the early part of May, was 26-year old, Felicity Hanbury, who arrived to take up her position as Deputy Officer in Charge of the WAAF Section as Assistant Section Officer. She had served briefly in the Auxiliary Transport Service before entering into the Royal Air Force as an Aircraftswoman Equipment Assistant 2nd Class. After taking various courses and promotions, she was posted on cypher duties to No. 30 Group Headquarters at Kelvin House in London. In personal life, she had married Jock Charles Mackenzie Hanbury, a RAF Officer Pilot in 1935; he was serving with No. 615 Squadron based at RAF Kenley, when he was tragically killed in a Gloster Gladiator N2314 in a night-flying accident on 1st October 1939, when his aircraft flew into the ground at Beare Green, south of Dorking, Surrey, leaving Felicity as a widow at the age of 25. She would later recall her first impressions of Biggin Hill:

> It was a lovely warm sunny day when I arrived at my new posting. The view over the officers' mess terrace was one of the best views looking over the countryside of Kent. The aerodrome itself was in immaculate condition especially the station's gardens that were all perfectly trimmed. My responsibility was second in command to over 250 WAAFs, the officer in charge being Section Officer A. F. Nicholl. We lived in our own Officers' mess in a married quarter that had previously been used by the station commander. During the following weeks, the airwomen practised air-raid shelter drill

and anti-gas practice in addition to their normal duties.

'B' Flight of No. 79 Squadron moved down to Manston aerodrome to carry out patrols between the 6th and the 10th May, and then returned to Biggin Hill; when the entire squadron received orders to go to France. The ground personnel were transported that afternoon by Bombay and Ensign Transport aircraft and arrived at Merville at 5.00 pm. Their Hurricanes followed at between 6.00 and 8.00 pm and all landed safely at Mon-en-Chaussee, except for three who landed elsewhere. Their place being taken by No. 610 'County of Chester' Squadron, who flew into Biggin Hill from their base up in Prestwick to begin operations. They were led by Squadron Leader Alexander Lumsden Franks AFC, an Irishman who was a pre-war regular officer who had trained at RAF Cranwell. He was known as 'Bonzo.' The squadron's radio call-sign was 'Dogrose.'

On 10th May 1940, Germany finally unleashed its Blitzkrieg attack, coming through the forests of the Belgian Ardennes, catching the Allies totally unaware and unprepared for the fast moving Panzer Tank Divisions and advanced Luftwaffe strikes, which overran every Allied position barring their way. Although the French and British Armies fought hard to stem the German advance and fighting was fierce in many places, it seemed almost impossible to launch any organised counter-attacks. Communication between the armies was fragmented and no sooner was a position set up to defend, the Germans had already by-passed it or it had been taken through force. Peter Brothers flying with 32 Squadron remembers the first operation he carried out the following day, after the German invasion:

> I was a flight commander with No. 32 Squadron at Biggin Hill and had been with the squadron since 1936, which was an advantage as I had acquired quite a reasonable amount of experience when the balloon went up on May 10th 1940. We had just got a new commanding officer named John Worrall, he had just taken over from Squadron Leader Chignall on 6th May, and he asked me to

lead the squadron as he was brand new; on our first raid against the airfield near The Hague, at Ypenburg on 11th May. We were told to go and ground-strafe it, because the Germans had landed troops there. When we arrived over it, we found that the airfield was lit up with burning transport aircraft, all of which were burnt out in the middle of the field, clearly the airfield had been re-taken by the Dutch military and had destroyed the Junker Ju52s. We searched around for something to shoot at and found a Ju52 in good order hidden between a couple of hangars. We swooped in and fired several bursts from our machine guns and set it on fire. This later proved to have been a very unpopular thing to have done, because the Dutch had kept this aircraft intact, so they could use it later to escape to England in. But we didn't hear about this until sometime later.

Douglas 'Grubby' Grice also flew on this operation to Holland that day, his memories relate the following:

I remember our first major operation, which was to take-off and fly over Holland and attack the German aircraft which had landed at the Hague aerodrome. So off we went, we were excited, but how green we were; we flew at 10,000 feet, well within anti-aircraft range, but it didn't seem to worry anyone. We were equipped with maps that measured two-feet square, which covered the whole of Europe, so Holland covered about two inches and although you could see The Hague, where was the airfield? We flew around and eventually found the airfield and decided to dive down in squadron formation; as we got lower we noticed that there was a few aircraft still intact and few that had burnt out. We flew low over the aerodrome and were not met by any enemy fire, so we headed back for home. On our arrival back at Biggin we were told that the aerodrome had been recaptured by the Dutch forces a few hours before we got there, and they had set fire to all the Junkers Ju52s that had landed there. So that was a very abortive trip.

On 15th May, British communications relayed the news that Holland had surrendered at 11.00 am following the devastation which had befell the city of Rotterdam. 20,000 buildings had been laid waste by the German bombing and artillery and 1,000 civilians had lost their lives.

In France the situation worsened when German Panzers had broken through and taken the bridges over the Meuse River and at Sedan the front line had been breached and the Germans were now pouring through. With many civilians packing the roads seeking refuge, re-enforcements were unable to travel and had to cut across the French countryside to try and get to suitable defensive positions. The advancing Germans had no such compassion and sent ahead their dreaded screaming Stuka dive-bombers and fighter aircraft to strafe the fleeing refugees who blocked the roads, causing them to jump into the side ditches to avoid bombs and bullets; many were slaughtered in this way.

Air Chief Marshal Sir Hugh Dowding Commander-in-Chief of RAF Fighter Command wrote in his letter of 16th May 1940 to Prime Minister Winston Churchill advising him of the present state of RAF Fighter Command and the call not to send any further RAF aircraft to France.

Sir,

I have the honour to refer to the very serious calls which have recently been made upon the Home Defence Fighter Units in an attempt to stem the German invasion on the Continent.

2. I hope and believe that our Armies may yet be victorious in France and Belgium, but we have to face the possibility that they may be defeated.

3. In this case I presume that there is no one who will deny that England should fight on, even though the remainder of the Continent of Europe is dominated by the Germans.

4. For this purpose it is necessary to retain some minimum fighter strength in this country and I must request that the Air Council will inform me what they consider this minimum strength to be, in order

that I may make my dispositions accordingly.

5. I would remind the Air Council that the last estimate which was made as to the force necessary to defend this country was 52 Squadrons, and my strength has now been reduced to the equivalent of 36 Squadrons.

6. Once a decision has been reached as to the limit on which the Air Council and the Cabinet are prepared to stake the existence of the country, it should be clear to the Allied Commanders on the Continent that not a single aeroplane from Fighter Command beyond the limit, will be sent across the Channel, no matter how desperate the situation may become.

7. It will, of course be remembered that the estimate of 52 Squadrons was based on the assumption that the attack would come from the eastwards except in so far as the defences might be outflanked in flight. We have now to face the possibility that attacks may come from Spain or even from the North coast of France. The result is that our line is very much extended at the same time as our resources are reduced.

8. I must point out that within the last few days the equivalent of 10 Squadrons have been sent to France, that the Hurricane Squadrons remaining in this country are seriously depleted, and that the more Squadrons which are sent to France the higher will be the wastage and the more insistent the demands for reinforcements.

9. I therefore request that as a matter of paramount urgency the Air Council will consider and decide what level of strength is to be left to the Fighter Command for the defences of this country, and will assure me that when this level has been reached, not one more fighter will be sent across the Channel however urgent and insistent the appeals for help may be.

10. I believe that, if an adequate fighter force is kept in this country if the fleet remains in being, and the Home Forces are suitably organised to resist invasion, we should be able to carry on the war single handed for some time, if not indefinitely. But, if the Home Defence Force is drained away in desperate attempts to remedy the situation in France,

defeat in France will involve the final, complete and irremediable defeat of this country.
I have the honour to be Sir,

Your Obedient Servant
H.T. Dowding
Air Chief Marshal
Air Officer Commanding-in-Chief

During the early hours of 17th May, the ground personnel of 32 Squadron were up at 3.15 am and began preparing the aircraft ready for their pilots to fly over to France to begin operations. They got airborne at 8.25 am and landed at Abbeville at 9.20 am; here the Hurricanes were re-fuelled as they waited for instructions. The airfield was already occupied by No. 615 Squadron, who looked a bit demoralised. Peter Brothers explains why:

> 615 Squadron were there at that time and they were in a pretty sad state of morale because the road was jammed up with refugees adjacent to the airfield, and what had happened was that one of their sergeant pilots had not turned up that morning. They looked around and found him in his bunk, lying on his back with a knife in his chest. Somebody had knifed him during the night. Whether it was somebody trying to rob him, a refugee or a fifth columnist they never knew, but it had certainly shaken the rest of his comrades. Anyhow we were there just for the day and did a few patrols and then got back to Biggin just after dark.

Another incident that took place at the airfield in France, which completely shocked the pilots of 32 Squadron, was when an enemy aircraft flew over the airfield whilst they awaited orders that day. Peter Brothers was there and remembers:

> I remember one of the days that we were in France, we had landed

and were refuelling, when we looked up and saw a Dornier 17 bomber flying overhead at about 2,000 feet and fortunately, he didn't take any notice of us, he was bound for somewhere else presumably. There was a French fighter aircraft doing aerobatics over the airfield, so we quickly approached the French squadron commander and asked to get onto the radio and tell the pilot about the Dornier 17 and get after it. Much to our surprise the squadron commander said 'This pilot is only authorised to fly aerobatics, not combat this morning,' which didn't impress us very much. They were wholly unhelpful, I think they were demoralised and they had very poor equipment in those days. Their aircraft were old fashioned and totally outclassed, their morale was totally non-existent and they had suffered terribly in the First War.

Douglas 'Grubby' Grice remembers one of his missions over France that month:

We were then sent on fighter sweeps over France to patrol St. Omer at 12,000 feet and it was on May 18th that we actually met the enemy for the first time, a frightening experience, well it was for me. It was a lovely day, the sun was shining with lots of cumulus cloud around; we had just skirted around some of this cloud, when suddenly in the distance there was a sight I shall never forget, the sky was full of aircraft. Within the space of a split second a Hurricane flew past me in flames and out of the corner of my eye I saw an Me110 climbing with a parachute wrapped around its tail, the poor unfortunate airman still attached to the parachute. I was looking up, back and sideways as I was very conscious that if anybody was going to shoot you down, it was going to be from your back. I then spotted a Messerschmitt 110, literally only three-hundred yards ahead and I had already switched my gun-button to fire; so I eagerly headed towards the 110. I thought I better have one quick look behind. To my horror of horrors there was another 110, three hundred yards behind me. Both of us were

> turning gently to the left, with him about to open fire on me. Well, you don't hesitate in those circumstances; it was a case of the control stick hard over, full right rudder and into a screaming dive in about a fifth of a second. By the time I pulled out, there was not an aircraft to be seen in the sky anywhere. Seeing no friend or foe in the sky and feeling very frightened and out of breath, I dived into the nearest cloud to get my breath back and after a few minutes headed back to base.

Elements of the German 1st Panzer Division had reached the French coast by 19th May. General Gort commander of the British Expeditionary Force no longer thought the battle to defend France was possible and in a message to the War Office that day he concluded that the Army must be evacuated if possible, before all was lost.

On the 19th, 32 Squadron was again in the action; taking off for Merville at 7.45 am and landing at the French airfield for re-fuelling before undertaking a patrol line between Lille and Valenciennes at midday, which turned out to be uneventful. During the afternoon, they patrolled between Cambari and Bailnciennes and it was while over the Foret de Mormal, they sighted a formation of 23-Messerschmitt Bf109s plus Messerschmitt Bf110s escorting a number of enemy bombers. Led by Flight Lieutenant Peter Brothers, the Hurricanes went into the attack and combat was met at 14,000 feet. Brothers recalls:

> The second patrol of the day we did from Merville, we stumbled across a bunch of 109s flying in precisely the opposite direction. One of them whizzed over the top of my head so close that you could see the oil streaks on the bottom of his aeroplane. I had this sudden realisation that this was the enemy and then the combat started and I managed to shoot one of them down. But one was quite startled by the whole thing at that stage.
>
> The Messerschmitt that had passed over my head went into a steep turn and he came round in a great curve and I was on the inside of the curve, and as the Hurricane could turn much better

> than the 109; I got him in my sights and fired. He caught fire and went down through the clouds, burning merrily. My first feelings were that this is going to annoy the rest of his friends, so I better look out, where are they. I searched the sky and found I was quite alone, so I headed for home.
>
> I think one of the things, that was the saviour of my life, was that when I first joined the air force, we were lectured by a chap called 'Taffy' Jones, who was a First World War ace of some renown. He stuttered terribly, and he warned us that there was going to be another war and that we were going to be in it. He said 'when you get into your f-f first fight, you will be f-f f****** frightened, but never forget that the chap in the other cockpit is twice as f-f f****** frightened as you are. This was a very good morale booster; I came to the conclusion that this German was as frightened as I had been.

Brothers had claimed his first victory of the war. His victim had been Feldwebel Heinz Pohland of I(J)/LG2, who had fortunately managed to bale-out and landed unhurt before being captured by the French.

During this encounter with the enemy, the squadron claimed six 109s and one 110 destroyed and a Dornier 17 bomber probably destroyed. The squadron suffered one pilot loss, that of Pilot Officer John Milner whose Hurricane N2462 was seen going down in flames, but a parachute was observed floating down. Following the day's activities in France the squadron flew back to Biggin, where they learned from their Intelligence Officer Flying Officer Sir Richard 'Bart' Leighton, that their comrade John 'Millie the Moocher' Milner had indeed escaped his blazing Hurricane and had landed safely, but had been picked up by the Germans and was now a prisoner of war. Douglas Grice recalls:

> Unfortunately, my particular pal, 'Millie the Moucher' had not been so lucky, he had been shot down and for him five years as a prisoner of war lay ahead. The unfortunate thing for him was that he was borrowing a pair of shoes of mine, which was one size too

small for him.

As the situation on the ground worsened, as the German advance continued and the Allies seemed to have no effective defence against the Panzer Divisions and troops, who were well supported with superior airpower, the allied air forces began to see their airbases soon over-run. On 20th May, Vice Admiral Sir Bertram Ramsey, a Flag Officer Commanding Dover, was charged with the task of organising a possible evacuation of the British Expeditionary Force under the code-name Dynamo, as the army retreated towards the Channel ports. The chances of being able to re-fuel the Hurricane fighter aircraft over in France began to be very limited as Peter Brother's remembers:

> It was pretty chaotic; we did a patrol over Lille and finished up landing to refuel at Dieppe. Again, a very tiny airfield, communications were appalling, we couldn't get any instructions from anybody; we were trying to get instructions from our headquarters to find out what they wanted us to do. We had to refuel our own aircraft from Jerry cans and having to start them ourselves, starting our Hurricanes on starting handles. I would get into my aircraft and get the chaps to start winding, once my aircraft was running I would get out of the cockpit and go and help the next pilot start his up and so on, until we were ready to take-off. There was no food available, we had to beg food from the local farm nearby, we managed to get our hands on a loaf of bread, but that was about it. It was a scene of general chaos and this went on I suppose until about the 21st May, when they final cancelled all the trips to France. We then operated from our home base at Biggin Hill or our forward airfield at Hawkinge.

No. 610 Squadron had flown five sorties by the early evening of the 21st May and at 7.20 pm received instructions to patrol between Calais and Boulogne to provide protection over the beaches and for the ships against bombing attacks. They sighted fourteen twin–engine aircraft approaching from the east, just off Cap Gris Nez. Squadron Leader

Franks positioned his men for astern attack and led Red Section in towards the aircraft. Franks opened fire on the aircraft, but the Spitfires of Yellow, Blue and Green Sections did not follow him in; Yellow 1 Flight Lieutenant Andrew Smith recognised the aircraft as not German, but in fact RAF Bristol Blenheims and he called over his radio to break off the attack. It was later confirmed that they were Blenheims on patrol and that a mistake had been made in recognition due to the failing light and thick haze over the coast.

The Blenheim MkIV, Serial No. L9185 that was attacked belonged to No. 18 Squadron based at Watton. It had been returning from bombing enemy troops near Etaples. Due to the damage that Squadron Leader Franks had inflicted, the pilot Pilot Officer V. Rees had to force-land the Blenheim at Wimereux. None of crew of three was injured and they made their way back across the Channel aboard HMS *Whitshed*

During a patrol on 22nd May, 32 Squadron were ordered to patrol with 601 Squadron between Arras and Merville during that evening and met with Messerschmitt 109s over Arras at 8.00pm. During this encounter Sergeant Guy Turner in Hurricane N2657 was hit by enemy fire near St. Omer, but he was able to force-land his aircraft and make his way back to the squadron , where he later filed the following report:

> The squadron was engaged with six 109s, with nine more approaching from the east. I left my squadron to attack the latter, but was shot in the engine by cannon fire at a range of 800 yards. The cannon fire appeared to be similar to a green Very light emerging from the starboard wing close to the fuselage. I took evasive action after I was hit doing a vertical dive, my engine stopped at 9,000 feet. I landed with my undercarriage in the up position near to Tourneham, about twenty miles east of Calais. It appears very noticeable in France that all enemy aircraft keep away while we undertake fighter patrols, but immediately the latter return to refuel, the enemy bombers take advantage of this to come over and bomb.

The squadron undertook two patrols the following day of 23rd, one during the early morning, which no enemy contact was made and the second at around 1.00 pm, when 'B' Flight was asked to provide cover for a Blenheim reconnaissance sortie. At 1.10 pm, the formation sighted eighteen Messerschmitt 110 twin-engine fighters near Ypres, Belgium and whilst climbing to engage, they were in turn attacked from an unseen formation of around fourteen 109s.

The combat was fast and furious with aircraft being thrown around the sky. The flight accounted for four of the German aircraft as destroyed and a couple damaged, but lost Sergeant Gareth Norwell who had joined 32 Squadron from 87 Squadron only a couple of days earlier, having already claimed eight enemy aircraft destroyed to his credit.

He baled-out from his Hurricane P3550 near Stavele-Brug at Beveren, north-west of Ypres. Wounded in the right arm and ankle, and suffering burns, he was transported to Calais and back to England, where he was hospitalised in the Pindersfield Casualty Hospital in Wakefield, Yorkshire. He did not return to flying duties until late 1941; when he was sent to Biggin Hill with the rank of warrant officer undertaking fighter control duties.

It had been Norwell who had first sighted the 109s coming into attack and his later report tells what happened next:

> Everybody did a right turn with the obvious intention of attacking the 109s, which left me wide out and well behind. There were six 109s coming up from the rear, I notified our leader and turned to attack. The first 109 went well above me and turned on its back. I put my nose up and gave him a good burst of fire as he passed me and he continued on his way upside down with smoke pouring from him.
>
> I stall turned off my attack and on levelling out I saw four 109s diving at me from the front. I saw no means of avoiding their attacks, so I lifted my aircraft's nose and got in a short burst on the leading 109 before I was hit by cannon fire in the right arm. My machine burst into flames and I succeeded in getting out and

taking to my parachute. I was fired at and hit in my right ankle by the French, before they realised their mistake and on landing packed me off to hospital.

That same day, a signal was received giving orders that No. 79 Squadron was to return home from their base in France to Biggin Hill, the majority of the personnel sailing back on the SS *Biarritz*. One squadron which now came under the control of Biggin Hill was No.242 (Canadian) Squadron; who had arrived at the aerodrome the previous day. Their radio call-sign was 'Lorag'

The squadron had already sent a detachment of ten pilots from 'A' Flight on 16th May, to fly alongside No. 607 and 615 Squadrons. Commanded by Squadron Leader Fowler Morgan Gobeil, the Canadians flew their first mission over France patrolling between Arras, Albert and Frevent during the afternoon and encountered a trio of German reconnaissance aircraft, Henschel He126s. These fell quickly to the guns of Flight Lieutenant D. Miller and a shared kill between Pilot Officers Stansfield and MacQueen. The third claim was made by Flying Officer Graafstra and Flying Officer Madore.

The next morning at 7.30 am, the squadron took off from the forward base at Manston and had been given the task of escorting a Blenheim on a reconnaissance flight over Cambrai, but during the flight they were attacked by 10 Messerschmitt 109 fighters of I/JG1. No.242 came off second best and suffered four casualties; Pilot Officer John Benzie was wounded and forced to bale-out of his Hurricane P2550, south-west of Ypres, he eventually made his way to Dunkirk and back to Britain.

Flying Officer John W. Graafstra was shot down and killed in Hurricane P2809 over Douai, his aircraft crashing near Wancourt, Pilot Officer Garfield A. Madore suffered the same fate and his aircraft P2730 crashed and exploded on impact at Sailly-sur-Lys, south-west of Ypres. Hurricane P3392 was also shot down, but its pilot, Pilot Officer J.W. Smiley although suffering from a wound to the head was able to take to his parachute as his aircraft fell to earth, crashing at Ecques, south of St Omer. Smiley was captured when he landed. Both Benzie and

Madore had been the victims of the German ace Hauptmann Wilhelm Balthasar.

The 24th May, was another bad day for 242 Squadron, whilst on patrol during the morning between Dunkirk and St.Omer; as the Hurricane were returning a German anti-aircraft battery opened fire on them as they flew over. In turning to avoid the gunfire, two of the Hurricanes collided; P3266 flown by Pilot Officer Robert L. Hill and P3272 with Pilot Officer James W. Mitchell fell into the Channel killing both men. The next day, they flew two patrols, one in the morning between Calais and Dunkirk which was uneventful, then during the late afternoon between Ypres and Lille. It was during this sortie that their commander Squadron Leader Gobeil claimed a Messerschmitt 110.

Operation 'Dynamo' was implemented between 6 pm and 7 pm on Sunday 26th, when every available ship and boat was ordered to head for the Dunkirk area. During the preceding week many men had already been evacuated from Boulogne and Calais, where fierce fighting took place between the 19th and 26th. Peter Brothers own memories of this time recall:

> I think the first thing was the tremendous feeling about the troops stuck on the beaches and the dawning realisation that this was deadly serious. On one pass over Calais, there was the Rialto Cinema burning below, you thought my goodness, that could be Bromley or somewhere in England. We were sweeping mainly inland of Dunkirk, because there was no point waiting over the beaches for the Luftwaffe to arrive and do a bombing run, you wanted to get at them before they got there. I can't recall shooting down anything at that time, but there was a lot of activity.

On the evening of 26th May at 9.00 pm, No. 213 'Ceylon' Squadron flew in to Biggin Hill from RAF Wittering to take up position for the Dunkirk evacuation; led by Squadron Leader J.H. Edwardes Jones; their radio-call sign was 'Bearskin.' They went into action early the following morning at 5.45 am, when they carried out a patrol in company with six

Hurricanes of No. 242 Squadron between Ostend and Zeebrugge. This was as protection for shipping against enemy dive-bombing, but the patrol was uneventful and no German aircraft were sighted; although a large splash was observed off the Zeebrugge Mole.

Two more patrols were carried out during the afternoon and during the last patrol at 4.10 pm, the nine aircraft of 213 Squadron were patrolling between Gravelines and Furnes when they sighted ten Messerschmitt 109s. These were engaged with two being shot down by Flight Lieutenant 'Widge' Wight, one by Pilot Officer Atkinson and another by Flying Officer Winning. They suffered no casualties and landed back at Biggin at 6.10 pm.

By Monday 27th May, Dynamo was in full operation and the scores of 'Little Ships' were making many trips to and fro across the Channel. The armies on the beaches continued bravely to endure the Luftwaffe bombing, while patiently waiting their turn in the long queues to get aboard a ship and home to safety.

On this day, No. 610 Squadron was moved to Gravesend airfield to operate their patrols over Dunkirk, still under Biggin Hill's operational control.

During the early morning at 5.25 am, 213 Squadron operating from the forward base at Manston that day, were instructed to escort six Blenheims of No. 21 Squadron on a raid to St. Omer to attack German troops and patrol between Gravelines and Nieuport. The Germans threw up a very heavy barrage of anti-aircraft fire during the raid, resulting in the loss of two Blenheims.

While continuing to patrol, they observed a number of Heinkel He111s and Me109s and they went to attack. Flight Lieutenant Wight was able to claim one of the Messerschmitts as destroyed as well as sharing a probable on a Heinkel with Sergeant Butterfield. But in return they lost two pilots, Flying Officer E.G. Winning was killed in combat with the 109s of 8/JG3 near Ostend, his Hurricane P3354 crashing near Langemark, north of Ypres at 6.45 am. The other loss was of Sergeant T. Boyd who crashed his aircraft into the sea off Ostend. He was initially reported as missing, but was found later to have been rescued from the sea and returned to the squadron the following day. The remainder of the squadron landed back at base at 7.35 am.

After refuelling, re-arming and having a bite to eat, 213 were ordered to carry out a further patrol over the Dunkirk beaches at 10.00 am. The ten aircraft took off and headed once more across the Channel and after several sweeps inland from beaches at 11.45; they engaged a large formation of Ju88s, Heinkels 111 escorted by Me110s and 109s. At the end of the action, they were able to claim five 109s, a Me110 and a Junkers Ju88 as destroyed and another 109 probably destroyed.

Again the squadron did not get away unscathed; Sergeant S.L. Butterfield was shot down, but baled-out of his Hurricane P2721, landed safely in the water and was picked up by the passing paddle-steamer '*Sundown*' which was picking up troops, after which he was landed at Margate. Sergeant J.A. Lishman was forced to crash-land in the sea in Hurricane P2834, but although wounded in one arm, he too was rescued and on arrival at Dover was admitted to the Victoria Hospital. Sadly it was not the case for Pilot Officer Laurence Stone, who was listed as missing in action; his body was later found by the Royal Navy and he was buried at sea.

It was also on this day that the aerodrome was notified of the arrival from RAF Digby in Lincolnshire, that No. 229 Squadron would be operating from Biggin Hill and their forward bases. At midday, the ground crews of 229 were already on their way and at 4.40 pm, fourteen Hurricane aircraft under the command of Squadron Leader Harold Maguire had taken off and were heading south. Their radio call-sign was 'Keta.'

Flying with the squadron during this period was Sergeant Pilot Richard Ronald Mitchell from Parranporth, Cornwall. He had joined the RAF as an aircraft apprentice at RAF Halton in September 1930 and had worked his way through the ranks before applying for pilot training in 1938. Having gained his wings, he was posted to No. 229 Squadron in October 1939, then based at RAF Digby in Lincolnshire and equipped with Bristol Blenheim twin-engine aircraft. The squadron then re-equipped with Hawker Hurricane Mk1 fighters in February

1940. Mitchell recalls his time during the squadrons operations in May 1940, over France and Dunkirk

We were given orders to fly off to France to help out. One detachment from the squadron had already gone before us; we were ordered to land and refuel at Hawkinge, but before we took off we received orders to cancel the flight. This was due to Air Chief Marshal Hugh Dowding's refusal against Prime Minister Winston Churchill, to send any more RAF fighters over to France as the situation worsened.

We did a few sweeps over France patrolling inland from east to west and north to south. I remember we had the job of escorting some transport aircraft that was taking spares to Merville. We were told in our briefing that the transports would be flying at around 120 mph. When we got to Merville we was to stay there for ten minutes, which was all we could do, because of lack of fuel and then escort the transports back after they had thrown their cargo out. We were pretty green at that time, when we were suddenly attacked by 109s, which was to be the first time I had ever fired my guns in anger in a Hurricane.

We had been circling around the airfield as if it was peacetime, they jumped us and they must have been greener than we were because we lost only two aircraft, but the people on the ground reckoned that more had been shot down around the airfield, which must have been German aircraft. It was the first time in my life I had seen a Messerschmitt, and trying to shoot this thing down; I later learnt that a colleague of mine had shot down an enemy fighter which had got behind me on my tail. Most of us came back and a couple of our chaps had baled-out and turned up later.

We moved to Biggin Hill with the remnants of a squadron, we hadn't got all our chaps back from France. We joined with other squadrons there and one day during the evacuation, we set off from Biggin Hill just as it was getting light, we had carried out three trips over there by 10.00 in the morning. We landed back at

Manston with only four aircraft of the twelve that had started, the others had landed elsewhere.

I remember that I lost a room-mate on that particular day. It was a hard introduction as we were not battle-hardened by any means. We had a little field-telephone at the dispersal there and when it rang, we thought they must be sending us back to base, but the officer in charge said 'sorry chap's we have got to go over again.' Most of the time we never got over Dunkirk, we would be intercepting bombers or fighters just out over the coast or inland.

I remember we were on our way to Dunkirk and were half-way there, when I was suddenly attacked by two Messerschmitt 110s. I did a steep climbing turn to the right to get away from them, then I heard a massive bang, thinking I had been hit, I went straight into a spin, I started to undo my straps and prepared to jump out; all I could see was the water underneath. But the aircraft didn't look too damaged to me though I was spinning down and lost at least 15,000 to 16,000 feet before I pulled out at 9,000 feet. I came out of the spin almost behind two Junkers 88s, so I fired my guns at one of them. I was convinced that I had hit it, but I didn't see it go down.

I returned and decided what I should do in regards to landing as I thought that my aircraft was damaged. I carried out a successful landing and got out, crawled around the Hurricane to see where the bullet holes had hit, but to my amazement I couldn't find any. I found out later that the bang I had heard was not due to enemy fire, but was due to a high-speed stall I had undertaken during the climbing turn.

No. 610 had not encountered the enemy all day, but on their final patrol at 6.10 pm, this all changed. Taking off from Manston they patrolled between Dunkirk and Gravelines and forty-five minutes later they observed an intense barrage of anti-aircraft fire between Bergues and Furnes, this ceased as they approached and they spotted a single Heinkel 111 at 15,000 feet heading east. Squadron Leader Franks dived down towards the bomber, but did not open fire. He overtook it to make sure it was an enemy aircraft, not wishing to make the same mistake he had done on 21st May against a Blenheim. He then ordered Flying Officer Smith and Sergeant Medway to attack. Smith fired all his ammunition at the aircraft along its starboard fuselage and engine, and on breaking away it was emitting flames and black smoke.

Three Spitfires from Yellow Section also attacked. As the Heinkel began to lose height it fired off signal flares, which suddenly brought thirty to forty Messerschmitt 110s down into the battle. Obviously the Heinkel had been used as bait to draw in the RAF fighters. The Messerschmitts of ZG52 had been waiting to pounce. A large dogfight ensued and 610 were able to claim several of the enemy machines, four Messerschmitts confirmed destroyed, three unconfirmed. The Heinkel of 3/KG1 managed to return to its base with just one of the crew killed. The squadron sadly lost two pilots in this engagement, Flying Officer A. Medcalf in Spitfire L1016 and Sergeant W. Medway in L1003 both failed to return and listed as missing in action..

Douglas 'Grubby' Grice of 32 Squadron remembers this period:

> For us Dunkirk was a disappointment, we only met the enemy once, while the other squadrons met the Germans every time they went over. I suppose the answer was that Fighter Command couldn't keep up constant patrols and there were gaps between patrols and in the gaps the German bombers came. Alternatively, you were flying at 12,000 to 15,000 feet and the bombers were either above you or below you or you never saw them.

No. 229 Squadron was quickly thrown into the action and was going to learn quickly about survival in the air against their experienced opponents. On the morning of 28th, whilst on dawn patrol over Ostend, they encountered a formation of Messerschmitt 110s and 109s. Sergeant Stanley Hillman was killed, when he was attacked by a Messerschmitt 109 of II/JG26, as he tried to make his way back across the Channel out of ammunition, his Hurricane N2251 was shot down south-east of Dover.

The next day could not have been any blacker for the squadron, when they lost a further three pilots during an afternoon sortie over Dunkirk. Bounced by Messerschmitt 109s of 1/JG2, Flight Lieutenant Falcon Clouston in Hurricane P3489 and Sergeant James Harrison in P2876 were shot down into the sea and killed; Hurricane P2636 being flown by Flight Lieutenant Patrick Browne was never seen again and was listed as missing in action. A further two Hurricanes were also shot down, N2473 flown by Flying Officer W. New, he managed to jump to safety in his parachute, Pilot Officer A. Linney also jumped from his aircraft N2521, and was rescued unhurt.

Sergeant George Binmore Johns was flying with 229 Squadron on operations over Dunkirk:

> I had served with a detachment of No. 229 over in France during mid-May, but as the Germans began to overrun France, and we had suffered losses, I was told to make my way back to England, which I did by boat from Boulogne. We then operated from Digby for a couple of days and then went off to Biggin Hill for the Dunkirk Operation; didn't do very much though.
>
> We didn't have the range or endurance. We would get there and shoot at something, it was then a matter of getting back before you ran out of fuel. I can remember one chap landing back at Biggin Hill with me; his aircraft had just landed on the runway, when it just stopped completely out of fuel. I know I lost my flight commander Falcon Clouston who was one of the bravest chaps I knew, and lost two or three good friends over Dunkirk.
>
> We always tried to get as much altitude as we could, so when we attacked the Stukas or 109s, we could dive on them, rather than letting them have the advantage. I remember having a bash at a Ju87, but I didn't hang around long enough to see what happened to him, because I had a Messerschmitt 110 on my tail. I remember having a dogfight with a Messerschmitt 109, I got a good burst into him, but his fate was unknown. On 30th May, I claimed a

> Ju88, and on 1st June, I attacked two Ju87s, but with no apparent effect. We were never aware at this time of the allegations by the army on the ground that they never saw the RAF giving protection over the beaches.

No. 610 Squadron was ordered to patrol Dunkirk at 4.45 pm, once over the French coast they decided to operate in formation of pairs. At 25,000 feet Flight Lieutenant Andrew Smith experienced icing trouble with his Spitfire and left for home, leaving his colleague Pilot Officer Keighley alone. Five minutes later at 5.40 pm, the remaining Spitfires were attacked by a squadron of Messerschmitt 109s and combat was met. Four of the enemy were shot down, one each claimed by Squadron Leader 'Bonzo' Franks, Flight Lieutenant Ellis, Flying Officer Chambers and Pilot Officer Sidney Norris. Two pilots were lost, who failed to return; Flying Officers G. Kerr in Spitfire L1106 and J. Kerr-Wilson in N3289, both shot down into the sea.

Following their return to base, they were given instructions once more to patrol Dunkirk at 8.00 pm. This turned out to be a disastrous flight for the nine aircraft that took off that evening. Firstly, Pilot Officer Norris had to return with engine trouble, then Pilot Officer Lamb suffered leakage of oxygen and he also had to return. Over France, Sergeant Jenkins was shot down in flames; it was believed that he could have been fired upon by anti-aircraft guns causing his Spitfire to lose a wing. He was able to parachute down into the sea and was picked up. Flight Lieutenant John Ellis had attempted to attract attention to the naval vessels below in regards to Jenkins plight, but was fired on by the ships. Squadron Leader Franks in Spitfire N3117 went missing from this operation and was never seen again. He was the victim of an enemy 109 fighter claimed by Oberleutnant Weber, the Staffelkapitan of 5(J) TrGr.186.

Squadron Leader Hector Macgregor had a very lucky escape on 31st May, when leading 213 Squadron over Dunkirk they were engaged in combat with 109s of III/JG26. Macgregor's Hurricane was badly hit and he was forced to bale-out of the aircraft. Unfortunately, he landed in the middle of a minefield and had to be rescued by the army. He was later able to get aboard a vessel and land at Dover.

Not so fortunate were Flying Officer W. Gray in Hurricane P3361 and Sergeant T. Boyd in P3419 both shot down and killed. Two other pilots were shot down, but survived. Flying Officer Robinson took to his parachute over Dunkirk after his aircraft P2763 was set alight, while Pilot Officer Wilfred Max Sizer crash-landed Hurricane P3424 just south of Dunkirk, both men were unhurt.

229 Squadron also patrolled over the beaches later that afternoon and lost two aircraft during combat with Messerschmitt 109s of I/JG20 and 110s of 5/ZG26 at 5.00pm. Pilot Officer V. Verity had his starboard wing aileron shot away and this caused the aircraft L1982 to go into an inverted spin. It was very difficult to get out of the cockpit, but he finally managed and opened his parachute and gently floated down into the sea, where he was rescued by a paddle steamer. The other pilot was Sergeant D. Edgehill, his Hurricane P3553 was also damaged, he was himself badly wounded; but in spite of this, he managed to bring his aircraft into land.

Both 242 and 610 Squadrons suffered losses during that day. At 5.30 pm two pilots of 610 Squadron were shot down, Flying Officer Chambers crashed into the sea in Spitfire N3274 and was never seen again. More fortunate was Flying Officer Keighley in Spitfire L1013; he was able to parachute down into the sea and was rescued and put aboard a vessel and landed back at Margate. Later during the evening at 8.15 pm, Hurricane P2732 of 242 being flown by Pilot Officer G. Stewart was shot down over Nieuport and plummeted into the sea, his body was never found.

As the operations continued over in France, the squadrons still continued to suffer casualties. On 2nd June, while carrying out a wing patrol over Dunkirk from Manston, No. 32 Squadron suffered the loss of Sergeant D. Flynn in Hurricane P2727, when he was shot down in combat with Messerschmitts over Dunkirk at 8.10 am. Luckily, he was able to parachute to safety, but was captured and spent the remainder of the war as a prisoner. 'Grubby' Grice flew on operations on June 8th, a day he was never to forget:

We had been sent to patrol Merville on June 8th, we had taken off from Biggin Hill at around 7.00 am and we crossed the coast at the mouth of the Seine at Le Havre. When suddenly two or three miles ahead we saw some Heinkel bombers with an escort of Messerschmitt 110s flying in a very loose formation, but above them were 109s. We swooped on the bombers; I was leading a section of three, Yellow Section. Red Section was being led by Michael Crossley and Blue Section by Peter Brothers.

By the time I was within half a mile of the bombers suddenly the 109s began to take a keen interest. So we had to break away and deal with the German fighters and with a little aggressive manoeuvring the two that had seen me and my section had lost heart and flown away. In the meantime I had lost touch with my No.2 and No. 3, so I was alone and had to catch up with the bombers.

The Heinkel wasn't all that slow and the Hurricane wasn't all that fast, so it took me at least two or three minutes to catch up, by which time the Heinkels which had been flying in no formation had got together and the nearest Heinkels were flying in Vic formation. Because I hadn't got the speed to climb up and dive down, I approached comparatively slowly from the rear and opened fire on the port engine of the left hand bomber and got it a nice long burst and there was a bang. Immediately, my cockpit was filled with vapour and my eyes started to sting and I could smell glycol. I knew exactly what had happened; one of the gunners from one of the other Heinkels had put a bullet through my radiator which meant the glycol was pouring out.

I broke away and looked at my oil temperature gauge and it was going up at a rate of knots, obviously all of the coolant had drained out of the engine, so being slightly afraid of fire, I switched off and glided in the same direction that the bombers were taking. The direction was due south and I knew I would have to make a belly-landing somewhere. I continued until I saw a nice large field and did a belly-landing, I got out and wondered what the hell to do, when suddenly a small French agricultural worker came running across the field, shook me by the hand, garbling away in French. I got out my map and asked in my schoolboy French, 'where is here? He looked at the map and his finger went all over it and then he suddenly put his finger on a spot which was not very far from Rouen, so I thanked him and at that precise moment a car drew up in the road near the field and a woman got out, which could have been the farmer's wife.

She walked across, started talking to me in French, which all went over my head; she motioned me to come with her and we got into the car and drove a little way and met up with the local police, the women spoke to them for a minute or so and told her that she better take me back to my aircraft. As it happened that was quite a good thing, because as it happened and stopped by the road near to my aircraft, two British Army chaps , one of them an officer, walking rather carefully around the Hurricane expecting to find a body near it. I shouted hello, and they turned around startled. We shook hands and I told them who I was and they said come with us. They took me into a wood, where there was a whole regiment of the British Army with artillery pieces.

Here I was introduced to the colonel and heard their story. They had had a miserable last three weeks, having to move by night and hide up during daylight and they were rather depressed. They offered me a car and driver to take me into Rouen, about twelve miles away; or to Le Touquet, where they were heading for. I thought it would be better to go to Rouen than go to the west and if I couldn't find any air force there, I could catch a train south. I arrived at Rouen and waited and waited, this was about 2.00 pm, not having eaten since early morning.

All of a sudden a service car appeared and pulled up. Two people got out, one an RAF Padre and the other a pilot; to see a friendly face was tremendous and to meet another pilot. His name was Edmund Sylvester, he was stationed in France with 501 Hurricane Squadron. He had been shot down too, the day before and had been taken to the town's mayor's office, where he had met the RAF Padre who said he would take him to his base at Rouen. But the aerodrome had been bombed by Heinkels and the squadron had left.

We drove for a number of hours, before deciding there was no hope of finding any RAF aircraft available to fly us back; so we stayed the night in Evreux and were having breakfast that morning, when we heard the noise of a lot of aircraft in the sky, Sylvester said they were German bombers when suddenly we heard the sound of bombs exploding nearby and the room began to shudder and shake. He suddenly said, 'come on quick' and dashed out to the carpark, he found a car which still had keys in it.

We were driving south and came across an airfield and on it was an aircraft parked up, we drove in and found out this was the headquarters of the RAF Expeditionary Force. This was under the control of Air Vice-Marshal Barrett and this was at Dreux.

The headquarters had of course been moving during the retreat nearly every day and had arrived here on June 9th. Sylvester was told where his squadron had moved to and he moved off in the car and I was left there having spoken to the air vice marshal, who said 'you're very lucky, a De Havilland Rapid has just arrived which will be flying back to England tonight and I'll put you on board, so you can get back into action as soon as possible.' About an hour later, I and a few others boarded this aircraft and off we went. It was piloted by a chap called Bill Ledly, who had been with Imperial Airways before the war.

We were half way across the Channel, when I was looking out of the window and we seemed to be flying in black cloud; after few a minutes I realised we were flying back the way we had come, and news came back from the cockpit that we had to head for Jersey because the pilot didn't like the look of the weather. The weather turned out to be the smoke from the French oil tanks at

Le Havre, which had been fired and the smoke was drifting across the Channel. We landed at Jersey; and stayed at a hotel at St Helier, but we didn't take off the next day for some reason, but took off the following day and arrived at Hendon on the Tuesday morning.

My parents had received the feared telegram from the Air Ministry stating that I was missing due to air operations and awaited any further news. On the Monday night they were greatly relieved to hear my voice, because I had rang them from Jersey. The day after my arrival back at Biggin, I learnt I had been awarded the Distinguished Flying Cross and a few days after that I celebrated my 21st Birthday. It was a hell of a month; I recall my Mess bill came to around two-month's pay.

On June 8th, 32 Squadron had also suffered the loss of two pilots killed in action. Pilot Officer Geoffrey Cherrington had been shot down over Rouen by Messerschmitt 109s of III/JG26 whilst attacking Heinkels of I/KG1. His Hurricane N2582 crashing at Fief-Thoubert, Saint-Saens at 9.25 am. His remains were buried alongside his aircraft, before being re-interred as an 'unknown airman' in 1941. The other casualty that day was Pilot Officer K. Kirkcaldie who was shot down and killed, again by III/JG26. His Hurricane N2406 crashed near Houville-en-Vexin at 9.30 am.

The squadron carried out a Wing patrol from Manston with 79 Squadron between Le Treport and Dieppe during the afternoon of 11th June and during this flight they encountered three German Henschel 126 reconnaissance aircraft, which was attacked over Dieppe. Two of the German aircraft were shot down by Pilot Officers Daw and Smythe. Sergeant E. Jones in Hurricane N2533, who was reported missing, he was found later to have made a forced-landing and was captured. It is not known whether his aircraft had been hit by enemy fire or suffered mechanical failure.

The final result of the Dunkirk evacuation had seen the rescue of 338,226 Allied servicemen, which would have resulted in the loss of so many soldiers that it would have been doubtful whether Britain could have resisted an invasion if it had come and might have seen this country call for peace terms. Although Dunkirk and the fall of France were seen as a devastating defeat, the spirit of the British people was still strong. Winston Churchill in his speech in the House of Commons on 18th June 1940 declared that Britain was now alone in the struggle against the Nazis. He went on to say:

> 'What General Weygand called the Battle of France is over. I expect that the Battle of Britain is about to begin. The whole fury and might of the enemy must very soon be turned on us. Hitler knows that he will have to break us in this island or lose the war.
>
> If we can stand up to him, all of Europe may be free and the life of the world may move forward to broad sunlit lands. But if we fail, then the whole world including the United States, including all we have known and cared for, will sink into the abyss of a new Dark Age made more sinister and perhaps more protracted by the lights of perverted science.
>
> Let us therefore brace ourselves to our duties and so bear ourselves that, if the British Empire and its Commonwealth last for a thousand years, men will still say 'This was their finest hour'.

Following the fall of France and surrender to the Germans, the RAF Fighter Command Squadrons had a brief respite to replenish some of the aircraft and pilots they had lost during that campaign. Between the 10th May and 31st May 1940 the Royal Air Force had lost in total 857 aircraft and 891 airmen, killed, missing or captured. Biggin Hill squadrons had claimed 56 enemy aircraft destroyed and 33 damaged for the loss of 19 pilots. Peter Brothers reflects on this period after Dunkirk and the operations they were asked to carry out:

> After France, we had a period of time from 10th June 1940 until the end of that month, when we undertook bomber escort for Blenheims attacking marshalling yards and we were also doing patrols at 15,000 feet along the French coast. The trouble with

these patrols was the Germans took no notice of you on the way in, but waited until you were on the way back and getting low on fuel and also the sun was behind you. They would then take-off and climb and attack you from behind with the advantage of the sun. Fighter Command decided to put a stop to these patrols as all we did was suffer casualties and did not have very much success. One day 'Stuffy' Dowding, our commander-in chief came down to Manston, from which we were operating that particular day. We complained bitterly to him and he grunted, but the next day the whole of these operations were cancelled.

Douglas 'Grubby' Grice recalls the operation on the morning of 27th June:

We with 79 Squadron had escorted some Blenheim's on a bombing raid, this was just after Dunkirk and we were coming back, 79 Squadron was flying as top cover and flying behind us and higher. We crossed the French coast on the way home and thinking that was that, when I happened to look behind and there I saw 79 Squadron about two or three miles away and 2,000 to 3,000 feet higher than we were. They were suddenly attacked by a large gaggle of Messerschmitt 109s and we were too far away to do anything about it, so we just carried on flying. Suddenly I saw the battle break up and one Hurricane was flying by itself homewards; suddenly I saw a 109 diving downwards on this single Hurricane. I shrieked a warning over the radio, but the Hurricane continued to fly straight ahead, so I turned around and from a distance of at least a mile I suppose, fired my guns across the bow of the Hurricane, to wake it up. Again the Hurricane just went on straight and level and I saw the 109 open fire and could see its tracer bullets. It fired just one burst and drew away and then the Hurricane just slowly rolled over and dived into the middle of the Channel. At that stage I had no idea whom the pilot was. When I arrived back at Biggin, we were told that the King was to visit and

> present awards to those that had won DFCs, of which I was one. As a group of us were chatting together we suddenly realised that Jimmy Davies was not amongst us and had not come back; and he was the only pilot who didn't come back. So he was the chap I had seen dive into the Channel.

Not only had 79 Squadron lost an experienced fighter pilot and leader, but also Sergeant McQueen, who had been hit by enemy fire, was seen to bale-out of his burning Hurricane and float down by parachute into the sea. One of the squadron's Hurricanes was circling over him and signalled his position, so the Rye lifeboat could pick him up, but when they arrived he was found to be dead.

During that afternoon of 27th June, Biggin Hill was visited by His Majesty King George VI, to present medal awards to those airmen who had acted courageously against the enemy during the Battle for France and over Dunkirk during the withdrawal.

The ceremony was held at 3.15 pm, outside one of the main hangars; where station personnel were lined up on parade. The King was accompanied by Air Chief Sir Hugh Dowding, Commander in Chief of Fighter Command and Group Captain Grice who stood next to a small table with a cushion upon which the awards had been placed.

There were six medals to be awarded that day; and as each recipient's name was read out by 'Dickie' Grice, they stepped forward in front of the King to attention, as he pinned on the medals. Those pilots who received their awards were Flight Lieutenant Michael Crossley, Pilot Officer Victor Daw and Flying Officer Douglas Grice, all from 32 Squadron, each receiving the Distinguished Flying Cross. From No. 79 Squadron was Pilot Officer Donald Stones, presented with a DFC; while Sergeants Henry Cartwright and Alfred Whitby both received the Distinguished Flying Medal.

As the ceremony came to a close, it was noted by his Majesty that one DFC medal was left remaining on the cushion. He was told that Flight Lieutenant James Davies had not returned from a sortie during the morning and was presumed killed or missing in action in Hurricane

Ground crew prepare a Hawker Hart aircraft for the Empire Air Day display held at Biggin Hill 1934. (Authors Collection)

A pilot of No. 79 Squadron climbs into the cockpit of an early two-bladed fixed – pitch propeller Hawker Hurricane in early 1939.
(Pathe News)

A Miles Magister trainer aircraft at Biggin Hill in 1938. These aircraft were used by the pilots to familiarise them with flying a monoplane before moving on to the Hurricane or Spitfire. It was affectionately known as the 'Maggie'. (Authors Collection)

No. 3 Squadron converted to Hurricanes at Biggin Hill in April 1939. Pictured is one of their aircraft, note that only one of the wings has a roundel. (Authors Collection)

This photograph was taken during the last Empire Air Day display at Biggin Hill in May 1939. During a mock-attack, Bristol Blenheims recreated the bombing of a bridge and were then intercepted by four Hurricanes of 32 Squadron. (The Press Association)

Hawker Hurricane L1662 of No. 32 Squadron is re-fuelled after undertaking a night exercise during 1939. (Imperial War Museum)

Pilot Officer George Olding who was killed whilst undertaking a night exercise on 11th August 1939, when his aircraft crashed close to the aerodrome.
(Colin Lee Collection)

A group of 32 Squadron pilots pictured by one of the squadron's aircraft. Within the group is Flying Officer Robin Buchanan-Woolaston (2nd left) who was killed on the same night as Pilot Officer Olding. The others are F/Lt Crossley 1st left, and Pilot Officers John Milner and John White.
(Bob Ogley Collection)

Hawker Hurricane L1707 in which Pilot Officer Reynolds was killed on 11th September 1939, is pictured at the Paris Air Show in 1938.
(Authors Collection)

Pilots and ground personnel of No. 601 'County of London' Squadron lined up at Biggin Hill for squadron photograph in September 1939.
(Authors Collection)

Flying Officer Max Aitkin of 601 Squadron pictured in relaxed mode. He was to have an outstanding service record during the war. (Authors Collection)

This strange contraption is a home-made armoured vehicle, it was hurriedly put together for defence at Biggin Hill, September 1939.
(Authors Collection)

A Pilot of 32 Squadron climbs from his Hurricane, while the ground crew prepare to re-fuel. Note that that they are wearing 'battle-bowlers' helmets.
(Imperial War Museum)

A Luftwaffe aerial reconnaissance photograph showing the aerodrome of Biggin Hill located in the top right hand section of the image.
(Authors Collection)

Sergeant E. Jones flying Hurricane N2533, was listed as missing following a patrol over Dieppe on 11th June 1940. It was later learnt, that he had made a forced-landing and was captured. (After the Battle Collection)

Flight Lieutenant John Ellis of No. 610 Squadron, pictured with other members of the squadron following his return after claiming an enemy aircraft over Dunkirk.
(Copyright No. 610 'County of Chester' Squadron Association)

Ground crew quickly refuel a Hurricane fighter aircraft of No. 32 Squadron at Biggin Hill for another patrol. Note the pilot is still in the cockpit. (Copyright IWM HU 57450)

Officers and NCOs of No.32 and 79 Squadron's stand ready to receive their medal awards from His Majesty, King George VI at Biggin Hill on the afternoon of 27th June 1940. Those pictured are: Pilot Officers Daw, Grice and Stones followed by Sergeants Whitby and Cartwright. (The Press Association)

Sergeant Sydney Ireland was tragically killed during a dogfight practice on 12th July 1940 whilst serving with No. 610 Squadron. (Colin Brown Collection)

Spitfires of 610 Squadron coming in to land at RAF Hawkinge, July 1940. (Copyright IWM HU 87412)

Pictured at Biggin Hill's forward base at Hawkinge, Pilot Officer Rupert Smythe of 32 Squadron is seated in his cockpit ready for take-off, 29th July 1940. (Copyright IWM HU 54417)

Flying Officer Douglas 'Grubby' Grice, tries to relax at Hawkinge, following a patrol with No.32 Squadron. (Copyright Getty Images)

This portrait photograph of Pilot Officer Keith Gillman of No. 32 Squadron was taken at Hawkinge in July 1940 and was used extensively in newspapers including this one on the front cover of Picture Post. Gillman was listed as missing over the Channel on 25th August 1940. (Authors Collection)

A smiling Pilot Officer Peter Brothers joined 32 Squadron at Biggin Hill in October 1936 and was an experienced fighter pilot and had claimed several enemy aircraft by the end of 1940. (Authors Collection)

Sergeant Tony Pickering served briefly with No. 32 Squadron in July & August 1940, before going to 501 Squadron.
(Tony Pickering Collection)

Pilots of 32 Squadron pictured in July 1940. Left to right standing: Pfeiffer, Humpherson, Gardner, Crossley, Grice and Pain. Seated left to right: Eckford and two Polish pilots; Pniak and Wlasnowalski. (Authors Collection)

The remains of the Dornier 17 bomber of 9/KG76 that crash-landed at Leaves Green, near Biggin Hill on 18th August 1940, shot down by Sergeant Dymond of 111 Squadron following the German attack on RAF Kenley. (The Press Association)

Two of the Luftwaffe crew of the Leaves Green Dornier. Left: Pilot Oberleutnant Rudolf Lamberty and Staffelkapitan Hauptmann Joachim Roth. All the five crew survived and became prisoners of war. (Chris Goss Collection)

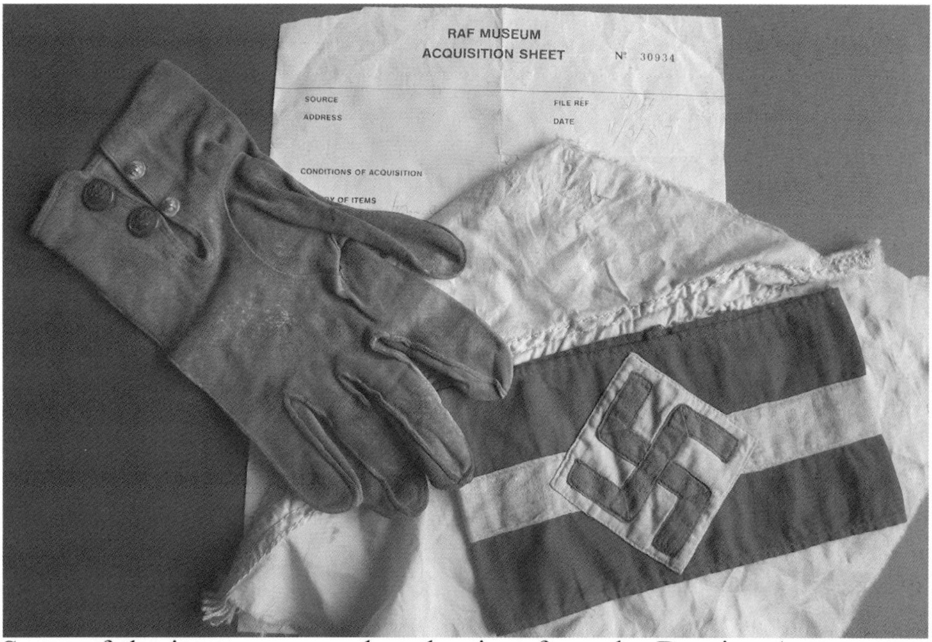


Some of the items recovered at the time from the Dornier. A crewmans flying glove, a Nazi armband and a piece of parachute silk.
(Colin Lee Collection)

Ronald Hamlyn of No. 610 Squadron became an ace pilot during August 1940. He claimed five enemy aircraft destroyed during one day of combat on 24th August, the only RAF pilot to do so in the entire war. He was awarded the Distinguished Flying Medal.
(Copyright No. 610 'County of Chester' Squadron Association)

During the attack on Biggin Hill aerodrome on 30th August 1940 by the Luftwaffe, this aerial photograph was taken by a German reconnaissance aircraft, and shows the bomb craters and smoke from bomb explosions still rising. The key on the bottom right gives details. (Bob Ogley Collecion)

P3591. Peter Brothers was on duty out on dispersal, the day the King presented the awards.

> I can recall one amusing incident that happened at Biggin Hill, it was when King George arrived to give out the awards to some of our pilots. I was in charge of the squadron, out on dispersal that day and after the presentation, the King was driven out to inspect us. He stepped out of his vehicle and with him was 'Stuffy' Dowding; I had the chaps lined up and introduced them to the King in succession. I informed the King, this is Flying Officer Gardiner and the King would ask 'how many have you shot down' and he replied 'two Sir,' I then moved on to the next pilot and the same questions were answered. We then came to Rupert Clerke' how long have you been in the squadron,' asked the King. 'Two years, Sir' 'How many aircraft have you shot down? None, Sir, but I was in Norway,' 'Oh' said the King, and they chatted about the Norwegian campaign, then we moved on to the next chap. I heard 'Stuffy' Dowding who was standing just behind us say to Rupert Clerke, 'why didn't you go down with the *Glorious? Rupert replied 'I'm terribly sorry Sir; I came back in a destroyer.'

The aircraft carrier *HMS Glorious was sunk on its return from Norway on 8th June 1940 by the German battle-cruisers Scharnhorst and Gneisenau with the loss of 1,200 lives.

For the remaining few days of June, the squadrons continued to patrol just over the English coastline, but no enemy aircraft were encountered. It was a quiet period as Britain and its military forces awaited Hitler's next move. This quiet time enabled the Royal Air Force to replenish the many aircraft and pilots it had lost during the French campaign, thus enabled those who had been on operations over France to catch up on some much needed rest.

# Chapter 4
# July 1940
## The Battle of Britain

On July 4th 1940, both 32 and 79 Squadrons were both heavily involved in action against the Germans. During the morning, a patrol was carried out at 10.05 am by seven aircraft of 32 Squadron led by Squadron Leader John Worrall to Le Havre, but no enemy aircraft were engaged. Peter Brothers remembers:

> The Battle of Britain was really a continuation on from Dunkirk, starting with the odd German aircraft coming over on reconnaissance or bombers making use of cloud cover to test our defences, many times we would be scrambled, but never saw anything. I recall, one day we did make contact with a Dornier 17, but we lost it in cloud.

During the afternoon at 2.00 pm, No. 79 Squadron took off to investigate a raid, led by their commanding officer Squadron Leader John Davies Clement Joslin. After only a few minutes they observed anti-aircraft shells bursting over the vicinity of Deal. Once over the sea, they sighted a convoy being bombed by a formation of 12-Dornier 17s at an altitude of 6,000 feet; they also had protection from above by Messerschmitt fighters. The Hurricanes went into attack the bombers, but had little effect before becoming embroiled with the 109s. On their return back to base it was noted that one Hurricane aircraft was missing, that of Sergeant Henry Cartwright DFM; an aircraft was observed crashing into the Channel off St. Margaret's Bay by the army. This was Hurricane N2619

At 6.30 pm, 'A' Flight of 32 Squadron were ordered off to patrol over Dungeness at 5,000 feet, during this patrol 'Green' Section were given instructions to join with 79 Squadron and intercept an enemy formation which had been picked up. As they approached, the RAF fighters were bounced by six Messerschmitt 109s at 6.40 pm. During this combat, Pilot Officer Smythe of 32 Squadron was able to despatch one of the enemy aircraft, sending it spiralling into the sea, while he damaged another, which set course back to France. Not so fortunate was Pilot Officer Grice in Hurricane N2463, who later recalled:

> We were in the air somewhere near Ashford in Kent and we were told over the R/T that there were Me109s beating up Manston aerodrome, so our leader turned and made for Manston; then I realised this was probably not a good idea, because there must having been a delay in the shooting on the ground and our hearing about it in the air and therefore the enemy would be on his way home.
>
> I took my section off to the right towards Deal and as it had been a very cloudy day, we were flying along at about 7,000 feet looking mostly downwards through gaps in the cloud, but always looking behind. I took one glance behind and there were three 109s, I suppose about 400 yards away diving down on to us and for the very first time in my operational life I froze, a most extraordinary feeling, I couldn't move except for my hand, which was moving the stick making gentle banks from right to left. I was looking straight ahead motionless apart from that. Of course the inevitable happened, there was one very large bang, my engine stopped, I realised I had no rudder control, no left hand aileron control either.
>
> My first thought was to bale-out, but by this time I was over the sea. The idea of baling out over the sea did not appeal, but in the meantime I was looking around madly. I managed to get the aircraft heading toward land, but I was losing height and I managed to undertake a belly-landing near to the golf course at Sandwich. That was really quite amusing as coming to rest, as

> I started to get out of my aircraft, the hedgerows erupted with soldiers headed by an officer. He came running up and stopped a few paces away and looked at me and said 'Hello Douglas, how are you.' I looked at him and said 'Hello Bill how nice to see you.' We had known each other as territorial soldiers years before and here he was guarding Britain with a few soldiers with few rifles and there was I, a stricken fighter pilot.
>
> I was quite unhurt so we had a quick chat; his troops were very impressed to find out their officer knew a pilot. We walked around my aircraft to inspect the damage, I had been terribly lucky, the shell that had gone through my port wing root had stopped the engine, two cannon shells had severed the elevator controls, so I was lucky to get down at all.

Pilot Officer Keith Gillman had also received damaged to his Hurricane N2724 and had to undertake a forced- landing at Hawkinge.

Ten aircraft of No. 79 Squadron took off on an evening patrol on 7th July at 8.50 pm to patrol Dover at 8,000 feet. Although no enemy aircraft were seen, on return to base it was found that Squadron Leader Joslin had not returned. His aircraft P2756 was found to have crashed at Chilverton Elms situated between Folkestone and Dover and he had been killed in the crash. He was buried at Buckden Cemetery near Huntingdon north of Cambridge. The job of leading the squadron was passed on to Flight Lieutenant Haysom.

The following day, 8th July the squadron suffered the loss of two further pilots whilst on patrol over Dover at 3.15 pm, when several enemy aircraft were observed and encountered. Pilot Officer J.E.R. Wood was shot down in Hurricane N3284 in flames by a Messerschmitt 109; he managed to bale out into the sea and was picked up by a naval patrol boat, but he had already succumbed to burns. Flying Officer E.W. Mitchell was also shot down, his Hurricane P3461 crashed at Temple Ewell near Dover. The aircraft burnt for over an hour after crashing and it was impossible to identify his body. Identification could only be made by checking the machine gun numbers.

The Hurricanes and Spitfires of 32 and 610 had also been in action that afternoon providing air protection over a convoy off Dover.

Ten miles out from Dover, three Spitfires of 610 Squadron sighted a formation of nine Dornier 215s and went into attack, but none were claimed as destroyed or damaged. Sergeant Else saw his comrade Pilot Officer Arthur Raven's Spitfire R6086 hit by enemy fire and watched as he ditched into the sea, five miles off Dover. Raven was seen to leave the aircraft and begin to swim; but he was not seen again.

32 Squadron came under a surprise attack by six 109s. Pilot Officer Rupert Smythe's aircraft was hit during the first pass by one of the enemy and had to break away and conduct an emergency landing back at Hawkinge. Pilot Officer Grice was able to get into a position on the tail of one of the Germans and followed it down to just above sea level firing short burst from his machine guns until white glycol smoke began to stream from the 109. He did not follow it to witness the final outcome, but claimed it as probably destroyed.

The very first day of the Battle of Britain is officially recorded as the 10th July 1940, the weather that day was not ideal, far from it, with rain and showers over most of the south-east of England and over the Channel. During the morning the Luftwaffe sent up their regular reconnaissance sorties. One German aircraft picked up a convoy at North Foreland and immediately radioed the information back to his base.

No. 74 Squadron flying out of Manston was on patrol and found a Dornier bomber with an escort of 20 Messerschmitt fighters protecting the aircraft. The six Spitfires went into the attack at 11.00 am though outnumbered and damaged the Dornier which crash-landed back in France; two Spitfires were damaged in the engagement, but were able to carrying out force-landings at Manston and Hornchurch, both pilots being uninjured. Biggin Hill's squadrons were at readiness; No. 610 were ordered off from their forward base at Hawkinge and intercepted Messerschmitt 109s over Dover at 11.15 am; during the encounter, the squadrons commanding officer, Squadron Leader Andrew Smith was hit in the port mainplane, he flew back to Hawkinge and landed safely;

his aircraft had a number of bullet holes, but it was repairable..

It was not until the early afternoon that the Germans launched an attack against a convoy (code-named 'Bread') sailing close to Dover. Just after 1.30 pm, the coastal radar at Dover began to pick large plots of aircraft forming over Cap Gris Nez in the Calais area. The information was relayed to Fighter Command Headquarters and quickly passed on to 11 Group.

They immediately ordered the scramble of five squadrons to fly to the area under threat. The first on the scene over Dover were six Hurricanes of No.32 Squadron from Biggin Hill, no sooner had they arrived over the convoy when they sighted a formation of 24-Dornier 17s with an escort of 40 mixed fighters, Messerschmitt 109s and 110s flying at various heights above the bombers. Soon after, the other RAF squadrons arrived and combat entailed. Because of the cloudy weather that day it was increasingly difficult for the British fighters to chase the German bombers who flew in and out of cloud to avoid detection. The other RAF squadrons who were involved in the engagement were No.54 and 74 Squadrons from Hornchurch, 56 from North Weald, 64 based at Kenley and 111 flying from Croydon.

The fighting during this engagement was over in several minutes as the German formation headed back towards France. The final outcome was the loss of one RAF pilot, Flying Officer Higgs of 111 Squadron, who collided with a Dornier bomber of 3/KG2 whilst trying to shake off an attack by a Messerschmitt Bf109 piloted by Oberleutnant Oseau of 3/JG51. His Hurricane's wing was torn off in the collision and Higgs was forced to bale out, unfortunately his parachute failed and he was killed. In return the Germans lost eight aircraft destroyed. Only one ship was sunk, the steamer *'Bill S'*.

The raids along the south-coast had not only been the Germans only incursions that day. Luftwaffe raids against Falmouth in the south-west and Swansea in South Wales, with bombing of merchant shipping, factories and railways. In all 30 civilians had lost their lives with many more injured. So ended the first day of the battle.

At 6.00 pm, on 11th, No. 79 Squadron left Biggin and flew north to

Sealand, but due to bad weather remained there for two days before arriving at RAF Acklington to take up their new position.

Squadron Leader Roger Frankland was the Sector Operations Controller at the aerodrome at this time:

> I was a Sector Controller at Biggin Hill, of which I think there was four of us, who took it in rotation to be on duty to take the orders from No. 11 Group Headquarters and pass them on to the squadrons to do what 11 Group had in mind. The orders we would usually get, gave the amount of aircraft they wanted us to provide, either a flight or squadron and either to go on patrol over maybe Maidstone or along the south coast, at various heights. We contacted them over the radio; of course there was no VHF to start at the beginning of the Battle of Britain, we had the old system of HF which was a very primitive form of ground to air radio and it was pretty primitive and rather difficult at times to control. It was bad reception compared to the clarity which came when VHF came in later on. You just had to grin and bare it; you had your signals officer trying the best he could do.
>
> I was an old man at thirty and most of the chaps you were dealing with were early twenties or less. Nearly all of us who worked as controllers were pilots, so we had a good idea what was going on in the air and you had to remain cool and calculated, when you were gathering the information off the plotting table. It became a natural situation to be able to transfer the information you saw on the board and to relay this to those in the air.
>
> I suppose one was working four hours on and four off during this period, I was controlling, when the first German raid came over the south-east of England and it was certainly a slight surprise, I mean the quantity of enemy aircraft. The raid itself lasted about an hour and a half, which meant we were two or three hours hard at it in the Ops Room. Once battle had been met, your other attention was drawn to other aircraft coming back, some shot up or contacting air sea rescue, as well as getting the ground

crews ready for re-fuelling and re-arming as soon as the aircraft arrived back at base.

Two days later, on 12th July, tragedy struck 610 Squadron when Sergeant Pilot Sydney Ireland was killed whilst undertaking a dogfight practice with Sergeant Horatio Herbert Chandler. Ireland in Spitfire P9502 was seen to have dived through cloud, but lost control. His aircraft smashed into the ground at Pitchfont Farm, Titsey Park, near Oxted, Surrey. Ireland had joined the RAF Volunteer Reserve and had learnt to fly at No. 5 Flying Training School at RAF Sealand in Flintshire, north-east Wales. He was of Irish stock and loved to play the guitar and rugby. He was buried in his home town of Newtownbreda near Belfast.

On this day also, the aircraft of No. 141 Squadron flew into nearby West Malling aerodrome from Turnhouse in Scotland led by their commanding officer Squadron Leader William Richardson, which came under the control of Biggin Hill Operations Room.

The Defiant aircraft had been designed as a bomber destroyer and had only been fitted with a four machine gun turret located behind the pilot; this was operated by a gunner. The aircraft did not have any forward firing machine guns and once the German fighters had recognised this, the Defiant was totally defenceless from head-on attacks or from below. 141's Maintenance Flight was based at Biggin, whilst the remainder of the squadron at West Malling, would use the forward airfield at Hawkinge.

It has for many years been reported that 610 Squadron suffered the loss of 22 year old Sergeant Pilot Patrick Watson-Parker on 13th July, carrying out a routine flight in Spitfire R6807. But there is no evidence whatsoever of him ever being with 610 Squadron and that he was not operational with the squadron on this date? Watson Parker had served with No. 263 Squadron based at Grangemouth and was flying Hurricanes during this period. Whether he was flying down to Biggin to take up a new posting with 610 Squadron or delivering the Spitfire when he was killed has never been verified. His aircraft crashed at Skid Hill Farm, Tatsfield near to Biggin Hill at 11.35 am. In the No. 263

Squadrons Operation Book, it mentions his loss on that date and does not say that he was a former pilot. So was he still on the squadron? New information now suggests that Watson-Parker was on detachment from 263 Squadron having had been sent to No. 6 Maintenance Unit at RAF Brize Norton in Oxfordshire as a ferry pilot, when delivering Spitfire R6807, when he was killed in the accident in unknown circumstances. He was laid to rest at St. Peter's and St. Paul Churchyard at Cudham.

On Thursday 18th July, Biggin Hill received information of an incoming raid and aircraft of 610 Squadron were ordered off to intercept. As soon as the enemy bombers were sighted, they noticed the bombers swing around and head for home. The Spitfires began to follow the retreating formation, but they were bounced by Messerschmitt 109s from above, who come down with the sun behind them. During the combat that ensued, 25-year old Pilot Officer Peter Litchfield was killed in Spitfire DW-T P9452, shot down by Hauptmann Tietzen of II/JG51, into the sea north of Calais.

Operationally, the 19th July was very quiet, 32 Squadron was ordered off at 3.30 pm and on entering over the Dover area had sighted a formation of Stuka dive-bombers attacking over the harbour with anti-aircraft shells exploding. The squadron was busy trying to avoid the anti-aircraft barrage when they were bounced by twelve Messerschmitt 109s and a series of dogfights ensued. The combat only lasted a few minutes before the pilots from the squadron returned to base and were able to make the following enemy aircraft claims; Squadron Leader John Worrall and Pilot Officer Rupert Smythe, a 109 each unconfirmed, Sergeant Henson, a Junkers Ju87 and Flight Lieutenant Peter Brothers and Pilot Officer Keith Gillman, a 109 each destroyed.

The patrol had suffered one casualty, that of Flight Sergeant Guy Turner, who had been shot down, badly burned he baled-out into the sea. He was quickly rushed to the Union Road Hospital at Dover. His Hurricane P3144 crashed at Cox Farm, West Hougham. Because of the severity of his burns, he was later sent to the Queen Victoria Hospital at East Grinstead to undergo plastic surgery.

Peter Brothers had landed at their forward base at Hawkinge to refuel and re-arm, he remembers an incident concerning one of the ground crew who was working on his aircraft:

> We had engaged a batch of Junker Ju87s who were bombing the harbour at Dover we intercepted them and we managed to shoot down several of them and some 109s. I returned back to Hawkinge and was in the process of re-fuelling, I was sitting in the cockpit, as there was no point in getting out as they were pumping petrol into the aircraft. Meanwhile the armourers were on the wing, replenishing the guns. A battle was going on overhead. I was watching this, when suddenly a Spitfire shot down a 109. The airman who was pumping petrol suddenly looked up and said 'ah, we got one' with great delight. At that moment, a parachute blossomed after the pilot baled out and with a look of utter disgust the airman said 'the jammy bastard,' which I thought was rather amusing.

That day, No. 141 Squadron who came under Biggin Hill's control, were airborne at 12.15 pm, when they were attacked by a formation of Messerschmitt 109s of 111/JG53 over the Dover area. Although they put up a brave defence against the German fighters, they were totally outclassed and decimated, losing six aircraft destroyed and one damaged with the loss of ten aircrew and two wounded. The squadron was quickly withdrawn from the fighting.

During the early afternoon of 20th July, 'Red' Section of 32 Squadron while on patrol sighted Messerschmitt 110 fighter-bombers attacking Dover Harbour. As the Messerschmitts dived to drop their bombs, Flight Lieutenant Michael Crossley led his men down and with Pilot Officer John Proctor destroyed two of the aircraft before they escaped back across to France. Later that afternoon, a merchant convoy code-named 'Bosum' sailing eastwards near Dover had been spotted by the Germans, who now launched an aerial attack against it.

Biggin Hill was ordered to send up standing patrols over the convoy for protection, 'Green' Section of 32 led by Mike Crossley was airborne and over the convoy by 5.00 pm. It was not long afterwards that the first enemy formation was sighted heading towards the ships. The German formation consisted of Junkers Ju87 dive-bombers escorted by a large formation of over fifty Messerschmitt 109s and 110s. Blue Section of 32 Squadron who were down at Hawkinge were immediately scrambled and some Hurricanes from 615 Squadron were also asked to help. Spitfires from 610 Squadron also received the call and headed towards the convoy to assist. The Spitfires had been flying a patrol at greater height and had the advantage over the German fighters. As the other squadrons engaged, they managed to destroy several of the enemy and caused some damaged to others before they fled back to their French bases.

Flight Lieutenant Brothers was leading 'Blue' Section of 32 Squadron during that afternoon; little did he know that the next few minutes would be so harrowing?

> I was leading Blue Section that day, when I saw a number of Stuka bombers start to attack a convoy off Folkestone. There was about 30 Messerschmitt 109s above on guard, so I climbed to attack them while Red and Green Sections went for the bombers. I attacked one Messerschmitt and set him on fire. As I got on the tail of a second, two 109s in line astern attacked me head on. A third was on my tail and a fourth was firing a full deflection shot at me from my right. I attacked the first head on and as they passed over my head, I turned steeply to the right and fired at the one on my right. Afterwards I tried to get on to the tail of the one behind me, unfortunately I lost him and as I finished all but about 20 rounds of my ammunition, I decided to circle round and try and get my section together. As I could neither find nor get in touch with them, I landed to refuel and re-arm.

Again 32 Squadron was able to inflict heavy casualties on the enemy, claiming two Me109s destroyed, three Me110s destroyed, four 109s damaged and one Junkers Ju87 destroyed. Sergeant W.B Higgins was slightly wounded during the encounter when splinters from bullets hit his bullet proof seat armour and ricocheted into his face.

Squadron Leader John Worrall leading 'Green Section of 32 Squadron had managed to damage two Stukas, before he himself was hit by 109 fighters of JG51 and was wounded slightly. His Hurricane was hit by cannon shells and bullets. In his report of the action he states:

> I attacked a third Stuka which also started to smoke, I was just about to fire another burst when I saw tracer going over my port wing. I immediately broke-away and felt bullets entering my aircraft from behind, which were stopped by the armour-plating. Then two cannon shells hit, one in the engine and one in the gravity tank. I had to make a crash-landing in a small airfield to the east of the aerodrome. Almost immediately she went up in a slow fire, giving me half a minute to get out.

They suffered the loss of one pilot, Sub Lieutenant Geoffrey Bulmer who had been posted from the Fleet Air Arm at the beginning of July, after undertaking a Hurricane conversion course at No. 7 Operational Training Unit at Hawarden. He baled out into the sea off North Foreland, but drowned; the victim of Luftwaffe ace, Oberleutnant 'Pip' Priller of JG51. One Spitfire from 610, which was flown by Pilot Officer Keighley, had its aircraft's tail shot away; although wounded, he had managed to take to his parachute and land at Lydden near Canterbury. He was the victim of Oberfeldwebel Schmidd of I/JG51

The weather was indifferent over the next few days and although the squadrons undertook a number of patrols, no enemy aircraft were sighted or engaged. At midday of 25th, nine Hurricanes of 32 Squadron were given instructions to provide escort cover with another Hurricane Squadron No.615 flying from Kenley, for a convoy (CW8) sailing west down the Channel. Forty-five minutes later while over Dover at 22,000 feet they sighted a formation of Me109s flying at the same level. Immediately Flight Lieutenant Mike Crossley who was leading went into attack the gaggle of enemy fighters and firing off a succession of bursts from his guns claimed one of the aircraft as probably destroyed. Crossley's combat report regarding the combat states:

> We wheeled round to the left to engage them; their leader turned and opened fire with cannon at me. But he was out of machine gun range and head on. I waited until I could fire and did so at 300 yards (firing 800 rounds) pulling sharply up as he went up over my head. I observed white plumes of petrol and glycol pouring from his wings, near the fuselage. This was confirmed by Pilot Officer Gillman (Yellow 3), who saw the enemy aircraft yaw away to the left and go down fairly steeply.

During this encounter Pilot Officer Victor Daw had become separated from the rest of the flight and ran into six enemy fighters, which he courageously attacked. In doing so, he was set upon by the 109s and his aircraft P3677 was badly damaged, he received a slight bullet wound to the leg, but he escaped and made a forced landing successfully near Dover.

610 Squadron were ordered off from Hawkinge at 3.00 pm as the same convoy was about to be attacked for a second time between Dover and Folkestone, as a formation of twenty Stuka's arrived escorted by fifteen fighters. 610 dived into the attack claiming four of the enemy 109s, only one being confirmed as destroyed.

Sadly, 610 was to lose their commanding officer during this engagement. Squadron Leader Andrew Smith's aircraft had been damaged during combat and he was struggling at the controls to make it back to Hawkinge airfield. In the process of coming in to land, his Spitfire's engine cut out, it stalled and crashed into a disused engine testing shed, the aircraft caught fire immediately and he was killed. He had been with the squadron since 1936 and had led it since the 29th May 1940.

They were again scrambled during the early evening at 6.27 pm and ordered to patrol over a convoy west of Folkestone, where they encountered another incoming raid in mid-Channel who was in the process of bombing the navy escort vessels. The interception took place at 10,000 feet.

Pilot Officer Stanley Norris shot down a 109 in flames and saw it hit the sea, Sergeant Horatio Chandler chased a 109 for five minutes and saw it go down burning. Sergeant Peter Else also chased an enemy fighter over Hawkinge at 500 feet, which was eventually came down in the sea off Folkestone witnessed by soldiers. Sergeant Claude Parsons placed himself on the tail of a 109 at 300 yards, opened fire for two seconds before seeing it dive vertically into the sea. Flying Officer Douglas Wilson's luck was also in, when he brought down another which was witnessed by Flight Lieutenant John Ellis. The final tally was five confirmed destroyed and three unconfirmed

There was a slight respite from the fighting due to bad weather on 26th July and the 27th, Biggin's squadron's only flew a couple of patrols and no enemy aircraft were encountered. No.32 Squadron saw the arrival of three replacement pilots who arrived straight from No.5 Flying Training School at Sealand. They were Sergeant Pilots Raymond Gent, Tony Pickering and Sidney 'Tony' Whitehouse. Tony Pickering would later recall his arrival and on meeting Squadron Leader John Worrall:

> The three of us arrived at the aerodrome and were told we would be flying Hurricanes. The squadron commander interviewed the three of us and said 'Pickering how many hours have you done on Hurricanes, what is your experience? I said 'I've never even seen one Sir.' He said 'you'll see one this afternoon and will do three circuits and bumps on the aerodrome and tomorrow morning at five o'clock you will be awoken at the Sergeants' Mess and you will be given a little breakfast, then taken down to the dispersal, where the Hurricanes are. We will get off the ground soon after light, at around six o' clock; we will then fly to Hawkinge on the coast.

John Worrall decided that the three pilots would have little chance against the experienced Luftwaffe pilots, so he sent them to No. 6 Operational Training Unit on attachment to gain more flying hours on Hurricanes. They would return to 32 Squadron on 25th August. Tony Pickering remembers his return to the squadron and the flights he undertook:

> Having gained further experience I flew with my flight commander, a chap named Hector Proctor, who three weeks before had been a sergeant pilot and had been promoted rapidly due to casualties. I flew with him and landed at Hawkinge and waited there for the Germans to come over. The flight commander said to me 'Pickering you have not flown other than yesterday afternoon, you will fly as my No. 2, do not get involved with any combat, you will not put your gun button on fire, your guns will be in the off position, you will fly immediately behind me within ten feet.' Later in the war, I realised why he had put me there. If anybody was going to be shot down it would be me. In actual fact, he was a good flight commander, an excellent man.
>
> Nevertheless, we did three trips from there with my guns in the safety position to get a little bit of experience. We did encounter the Germans, he fired his guns and we then landed back at base again. We did two days of that and then the squadron was moved north to Acklington for a rest period. The squadron commander then told us three new boys, were not in need of a rest, you're going to No. 501 Squadron at Gravesend. So that was my brief time with 32 Squadron.

Also arriving this day to take up his new posting with 610 Squadron was Sergeant Cyril Bamberger:

> I was sent to join the squadron at Biggin Hill on 27th July 1940 and interviewed by the commanding officer John Ellis, he asked me what I had last flown, which was a Hawker Hart and an Audax, both biplanes, and his reply was 'what the bloody use are you to me.' So I was packed off to the operational training unit at Hawarden to convert to Spitfires, there I did a couple of trips in a Miles Master, then on August 7th, I undertook my first flight in a Spitfire and did a number of circuit and bumps. I spent three

weeks there learning how to cope and gain experience on the Spitfire.

During the afternoon of 29th July, 'A' Flight of 610 Squadron took off from Hawkinge after an enemy aircraft plot was picked up over the coast. Once airborne they sighted a single Dornier 215 bomber, which on seeing the approaching Spitfires unloaded its bombs into the sea off Dungeness and turned for the French coast. The Spitfires attacked in succession, four of the aircraft expending all their ammunition on the unfortunate German; which was damaged considerably with pieces of airframe falling away and smoke pouring from its post engine. The bomber was last seen flying steadily at 50-feet above the waves. Later it was reported as being an aircraft belonging to Stab KG2, which crash-landed back at its base at St. Inglevert. Its only casualty was Leutnant Hunger who was wounded, but survived. It was claimed as damaged by 610 Squadron.

It was during this same day, that 'B' Flight of 32 Squadron who had been sent down to Hawkinge were to become the attention of press photographer of Fox Films, who captured the pilots relaxing at readiness and in the cockpits of their aircraft for an Air Ministry instructional film. The photographs were used in Picture Post magazine with the front cover showing a head portrait of Pilot Officer Keith Gillman in his flying helmet, goggles and his oxygen mask hanging loosely. Some of the photographs have since been widely used in many Battle of Britain publications.

The final action of the month came on 31st August, when 32 Squadron on their third patrol that day, at 5.30 pm, they received information over their radios of Heinkel 111s with fighter escort approaching just out over the coast. On seeing the RAF fighters, the Heinkels immediately turned tail and turned back to France. Not wishing to mix it with the Hurricanes.

So ended the first month of the Battle of Britain in which the Luftwaffe had attempted to knock out the coastal ports and installations. The next month would see the Germans try to knock out the Royal Air Force not only in the air, but on the ground.

# Chapter 5
# August
# 1940

At the start of August, the ranks of No. 32 Squadron were increased, when three Polish Pilot Officers arrived on 4th August, having arrived following a conversion course on to fighter aircraft at No. 6 Operational Flying Unit at Sutton Bridge. The men were Jan Piotr Pfeiffer, Karol Pniak from Cracow and Boleslaw Wlasnowolski. Although their English was not good, they soon learnt the main RAF slang for flying operations and were helped by the old hands of the squadron. They like everybody else acquired nicknames and were called 'Fifi, Vodka and Cognac.'

Polish Pilot Officer Jan Pfeiffer was lucky to escape with his life, when his Hurricane V7205 crashed 100-yards from the south-west boundary of the aerodrome on 6th August. His aircraft almost immediately burst into flames, but he escaped without injury.

Sergeant John Tanner who had joined 610 Squadron on 27th July was flying his Spitfire L1085 on a routine patrol on the morning of August 8th over Hawkinge, when he encountered Messerschmitts of JG51, his aircraft was hit and he was obliged to carry out a forced landing at Portmans Heath March at Wittersham. On landing the Spitfire overturned on its back, but he was able to clamber out without any injuries.

On 9th August, another foreign pilot joined the squadron, this was the Belgian Pilot Officer Rudolphe Ghislain Charles de Hemricourt de Grunne from Brussels, who had previously flown during the Spanish Civil War as a volunteer for the Nationalist forces and flown against the Luftwaffe when Belgium was invaded in May 1939. Peter Brothers remembers him:

Pilot Officer Hemricourt de Grunne was a Belgian and he had flown Messerschmitt 109s with the Condor Legion. When he came to us, he told us about the advantages and disadvantages of the 109 and how best to treat it. The advantages were its speed in the dive, its rate of roll in the climb, but it was poor in the turning circle and that its level flight speed was not that greater than the Hurricane Tactically, that meant if you forced the 109 into a turning battle you could turn inside them; or make sure that if they were above and came down that you could turn out of their line of fire. Sadly, he was killed in May 1942 when escorting some Blenheim bombers on a raid to Bethune.

During the second week of August, a change of tactics was initiated by the Luftwaffe High Command, orders were given to attack the Royal Air Force Fighter Stations and knock out the Radio Direction Finding Stations (Radar) situated along the Channel coast.

The task of knocking out the vital aerodromes in the south-east would then open up the opportunity to not only destroy the RAF Fighters in the air, but cripple them on the ground. Once this was done, the invasion could start in earnest.

Early morning of 11th saw both 32 and 610 Squadrons extremely busy as enemy plots were received in the operations room. No. 32 were first off being scrambled at 7.40, and sent to patrol the area between Dover and Deal. They sighted nine Messerschmitt 109s and engaged with them, but only one of the German aircraft was claimed as damaged, the others escaping back across the Channel. The squadron landed back at Biggin with no casualties to themselves. At 10.00, both squadrons were sent off once again as the alarm bells sounded that another raid was heading in over the Dover area.

Again a formation of Messerschmitt 109s was encountered by 32 Squadron and 610. During the engagement one German aircraft was claimed as damaged by Flying Officer Peter Gardner of 32 Squadron, while 610 claimed a 109 destroyed; but they suffered the loss of two pilots killed; Sergeants William Neville in Spitfire R6918 and John Tanner in R6630, who had followed the 109s back across the Channel towards Calais. Neville's body was never found, but Tanners was washed ashore and buried at the Southern Cemetery in Calais. Peter Brothers remembers those skirmishes:

> After a combat, you usually got split up all over the sky and I remember I was on my own, when suddenly I came across five 109s in a Vic formation heading for home and I thought rather stupidly that I could sneak up behind them and pick them off. As I gradually slipped up behind, I saw one aircraft suddenly turn away from the formation, I was not sure whether he had spotted me, but I came up underneath him and opened fire and all hell was let loose, because the four I had taken my eyes off spun around behind me. I took immediate action and dived away and headed for home rather smartly.

The first main attack by the Luftwaffe was scheduled for Monday 12th August, which involved attacking the coastal radar chain at Pevensey, Dover, Rye and Dunkirk. Three of the stations were hit, but damage was minimal and they were soon in operation once again. One bombing raid by Junker Ju88s of KG51 hit the radar at Ventnor on the Isle of Wight later that day and was put it out of action for several weeks.

On the morning of the 12th, whilst on patrol at around 8.00 am, No. 610 Squadron had sighted a low-flying formation of Messerschmitt 109s heading in across the Channel. They immediately went into the attack and forced the enemy to take evasive action, who then proceeded to head back home to France. Unbeknown to the pilots of 610, another group of 109s were waiting and dived down on the Spitfires.

During the engagement over New Romney, Flight Lieutenant Brian Bretherton Smith's aircraft K9818 was hit and burst into flames. He managed to bale-out, but suffered burns; he was rescued from the sea by a motor boat and admitted to Dover Hospital. Flying Officer Frederick Gardiner was slightly wounded in the leg by a cannon shell during the combat, but managed to crash-land his Spitfire R6806, sustaining further damage to the port wing. Spitfire R6621 also received combat damage, although the pilot did not receive any injuries, and

Spitfire P9495 landed, but was written-off as unrepairable. On the plus side Sergeant Bernard Gardner claimed three 109s destroyed and Pilot Officer Kenneth Cox another one destroyed and one unconfirmed in combat over Dungeness. Squadron Leader John Ellis 610 Squadron combat report for 12th August 1940 relates

> I was leading 610 Squadron, which was detailed to intercept a raid approaching Dungeness, when nine enemy bombers were sighted at 16,000 feet over New Romney in a very tight Vic formation in sections of three. The presence of the bombers was first noted after a stick of bombs was seen to fall into the sea off New Romney. Our height at this time was 10,000 feet. We climbed to attack the bombers which were flying towards Rye; we were then 1,000 feet below them and about 1,000 yards astern, when twelve 109s came diving down out of the sun on to our own tails. We were forced to break off our own attack on the bombers and a general dogfight ensued with the enemy fighters. We were told by our controller soon after taking-off that there we were to deal with the bombers and that another squadron above us would deal with the enemy fighters.
>
> In the dogfight, I chased one solitary Me109 flying very fast and diving slightly. He rolled on to his back as I opened fire and I continued firing as he started his vertical dive; I could see my bullets entering the side of his fuselage as I followed. I climbed up again to 15,000 feet over Dungeness and spotted another 109 climbing up into the sun. I caught him at about 20,000 when he started to spin down to the left, soon after I opened fire. I fired the remainder of my ammunition at very close range as he was spinning, but he presented a very difficult target. When I broke off my attack, his engine was ticking over slowly and he was still spinning violently and he appeared to be out of control. I left him to his fate and return back to base to re-arm. Flying Officer Lamb, who was behind me, later reported he saw this aircraft continue

> its dive into the sea and break up. I claimed one destroyed and the other as unconfirmed.

Later that afternoon, the first raids against RAF airfields in Kent was undertaken, Manston was first, attacked at 12.45 pm, followed by Lympne and Hawkinge. The damage caused was heavy, but the airfields were soon patched up and remained operational.

Douglas Grice of No.32 Squadron was in action that day and recalls the action before heading back to his forward base at Hawkinge on the Kent coast, and received a radio transmission from his controller on the ground:

> We were patrolling again over Ashford at 12,000 feet, when we were told that 20 plus bandits were approaching Deal from the east at 10,000 feet, we turned towards Deal and a few seconds later, we counted 18 Dorniers with a cloud of Me109s above them. Again in our innocence, we went around the front of the Dorniers and then dived on them from the rear and of course the 109s started to get busy, so we had to mix it with them for a minute or so, but they weren't really keen. I think we shot down a couple, I had to manoeuvre aggressively against one of them, but he dived away towards France, so I was left alone in the sky again with the enemy bombers steaming ahead. I was a couple of thousand feet below them at this time, so opening the throttle I went after them.
>
> They suddenly started to turn and I realised if they went on turning they would cross my bows about half a mile away. I did a sort of head on attack, but slightly to the side; I no nearer than probably one hundred yards, when I dived away, not wanting to be fired upon by the rear gunners. Meanwhile the port and starboard aircraft in the leading Vic formation of three had slipped away from the formation because they could see I was firing.
>
> Having done this attack I dived away, I was again 2,000-3,000 feet below the bombers going in the opposite direction and by the time I had climbed up again and at their level, they were still a mile

ahead and had bombed Hawkinge., which is where we had taken off from. It was quite useless trying to catch them up, then I heard over the R/T 'don't land at Hawkinge, airfield has been bombed.'

Having been very curious, I flew back to Hawkinge and there were considerable signs of bomb damage and the airfield seemed to have molehills on it. So I thought this looks interesting, I could see a path through the molehills and I landed and taxied between the mounds to where I had taken off from; a flight sergeant run over and said 'I think you better take off again quickly, Sir. I replied 'Why.' He said, 'you see all those molehills, there unexploded bombs.' I hadn't realised this of course, so I took his advice and weaved my way through the molehills and took off rather smartly and flew back to Biggin Hill.

Only one of the squadrons Hurricanes was shot down during that action; Hurricane N2596 flown by Pilot Officer Tony Barton; he baled out over Dover and landed without injury.

The following day, Tuesday 13th August was to have seen a more comprehensive attack by the German Air Force. Code-named by the Germans as 'Adler Tag' (Eagle Day) the raid was postponed initially during the early morning due to weather conditions and the raids did not resume until the afternoon, but weather still was poor. Dornier bombers did manage to attack RAF Eastchurch and destroy five Bristol Blenheim light-bombers, as well as damage to the hangars and block houses. In reality the day was a failure for the Luftwaffe, with the loss of thirty-four aircraft lost to thirteen suffered by the RAF. Although Biggin Hill's squadrons were scrambled a number of times that day, they were unable to intercept any of the incoming raids and no claims were made that day.

The squadron's had better luck on the 14th, when they took to the air at 12.30 pm and attacked nine Messerschmitt 109s of I/J626 north-west of Hawkinge at 16,000 feet. Pilot Officer Rupert Smythe was able to get on the tail of one of the 109s and shoot it down, the pilot baling out over the Channel. No sooner had Smythe finished off the 109, when he was attacked by another 109 and was hit in the glycol tank. With white glycol streaming from his Merlin engine, Smythe made a hasty retreat and landed back at Hawkinge aerodrome.

Tony Barton's aircraft P3146 was also hit, he had to undertake a force-landing at Hawkinge also. Polish Pilot Officer Boleslaw Wlasnowalski's Hurricane V7223 was also damaged and he landed in a field near Dover.

610 Squadron were also successful that afternoon claiming multiple enemy aircraft, when they engaged a large formation over Folkestone. Three Messerschmitt 109s confirmed as destroyed, two Junkers Ju 87 'Stukas' also confirmed destroyed, one Messerschmitt 110 confirmed destroyed, four 109s probably destroyed and three Ju 87s probably destroyed. Sergeant Bernard Gardner flying in the position of Green 2 was one of the squadron's pilots who attacked the formation of escort fighters consisting of twenty 109s. He was able to shoot down one of the enemy before he himself was wounded. His report of this action reads:

> I saw an enemy aircraft coming head on and firing. I immediately took evasive action and chased it to the sea, where I gave it one long burst of fire from my guns. Smoke came pouring out of it and I saw it crash into the sea. I then went to attack ten aircraft and received a tracer bullet in my left arm. I force landed in a field at Wye and was taken to Ashford Hospital.

Thursday August 15th was to see a number of raids by the Luftwaffe against RAF airfields. At around midday, Hawkinge, Lympne and Manston had received visits by the Germans, causing damage to flightpaths and hangars. Eight Spitfires of 610 Squadron was scrambled at 12.43pm, they sighted a formation of Dornier 17s and 109s ten miles south-east of Biggin. During this engagement two of the Messerschmitt's were damaged and one probably destroyed. During mid-afternoon at 3.00 pm, two large formations had been monitored by radar heading for the Kent coast. The first raid consisted of 100-plus and a second of 150-plus. A number of squadrons were called to scramble including 32

Squadron from Biggin. On this day 'Grubby' Grice flew his last sortie with 32 Squadron at 3.25 pm:

> I remember my last operational flight with the squadron. We had taken off from Biggin Hill to patrol somewhere over east Kent, when we were told to fly towards Harwich, as it was being bombed. We were flying at around 15,000 feet, I know I was using oxygen; we arrived over that area and saw nothing and we had just turned around and were coming back again, when at 4,000 to 5,000 feet higher we sighted a circle of Me110s. Our leader decided to take no notice of them and flew on and I was flying as what is known as arse-end charlie; in other words by myself at a thousand feet higher covering the rear of our formation.
>
> Suddenly out of the corner of my eye I saw a flash over my left wrist, and the next moment the cockpit was full of flames, the heat was enormous and I did two things instinctively. My left hand had gone to the handle of the canopy and my right hand had gone to the release on my harness and I was then pulling with both hands; the next moment I was out in the open air. I had made no attempt to jump out of my aircraft, I had been straining back from the flames while I had been doing a left hand turn, the aircraft had kept turning until it was on its back and I just fell out.
>
> As I was falling away, I remembered my parachute drill, which was to wait before pulling the ripcord; I waited a few seconds, pulled it and there was a sudden jerk and I was floating down with a marvellous canopy, drifting a couple of miles inland. Very shortly after that I was over the coast, a few minutes later I was a mile out to sea, then a few minutes after that about two miles out to sea.
>
> When the sea approached I was not the least worried because I was only a couple of hundred yards from a fishing trawler. I landed in the water, getting rid of my harness I looked round, there was the trawler and I waved like mad. I had tried to blow up my Mae West, but I was not terribly successful as something

seemed to have happened to my face with bits of skin flapping around my eyes, my mouth also felt very uncomfortable as if I had been burnt. I waved once more at the trawler as they had passed me by, what I hadn't seen was an RAF motor boat coming out from Harwich which was making straight for me. It eventually arrived and they hauled me aboard, that's when I began to feel rather sorry for myself.

We got back to Harwich, I was put into an ambulance and taken to the Royal Naval Hospital at Shotley, put on a bed then a nurse came along to cut me out of my uniform. I couldn't stop shaking like a leaf, I felt very embarrassed. The young nurse said 'don't worry; you are only suffering from shock.' I was eventually seen by a naval doctor, I was wheeled into the operating theatre, eventually coming to, hearing a voice saying 'it's alright Mr Grice, it's alright.' This voice went on and on, but what had happened was that the naval surgeon had cut away the bits of loose skin around my face, he had covered my face in a bandage, so I had a mask from just under my hairline down to below my chin. Of course I couldn't see anything, accept for a couple of holes for me to breathe through and a little hole where my mouth was. What they were frightened of was that I would come to after this operation, realising I couldn't see and start scratching at my face. They had put an orderly by my bed, telling him to keep on saying 'it's alright Mr Grice.'

Later on the air-raid sirens went off, a nurse came to my bed, saying that we had to go downstairs; I was apparently on the first floor, so being led by the arm, unable to see, I was taken downstairs by this splendid nurse, who herself was shaking like a leaf, not surprisingly with the bombs dropping not to far away. My fiancée at the time was Pam Beecroft, who worked at Biggin in the Ops Room as a Cypher Officer; she learnt of my predicament whilst she was ferrying some of the pilots to their dispersal. It had come as a bit of a shock.

A few days later they cut away a part of the mask, so I would be able to see a lot better. Then came the day, when they completely removed the mask so I wandered over to the mirror and had a hell of a shock, because my mouth had been covered in Gentian violet, there I was absolutely purple. I really was a sight, but I felt alright and was not in any pain.

Later I was seen by the top man Archibald McIndoe, who said 'that I was very lucky and that I would not need to undergo plastic surgery as the main reason was you came down in the sea and we learnt from you chaps that a brine bath was the best initial treatment for burns cases.' For a year or two I had a red line around my face, the part where I hadn't been covered by my flying mask, where I had been burnt, but eventually over the years it has faded. I never flew operationally after that, but returned once I was fit to carry duties as a controller at Biggin Hill.

During this action the Polish pilot Boleslaw Wlasnowolski in Hurricane N2671 was able to claim a 109 destroyed before he was also hit by enemy fire and had to make a force-landing.

The Luftwaffe were not in the mood for giving up and launched another raid at 5.00 pm; their targets being Kenley and Biggin Hill.

At 5.20 pm the pilots of 32 Squadron rushed to their aircraft, quickly strapped themselves into their cockpits and hurriedly took off, receiving information over the radio from ground controllers, who gave them a course and height to intercept the enemy. Nearing Selsey Bill, they sighted several formations of varying German bombers and fighters; Dornier 215s, Junker Ju88s, Messerschmitt 109s and 110s. Flight Lieutenant Mike Crossley would later report:

We sighted about thirty Ju88s accompanied by several 110s crossing the coast near Portsmouth, flying at 13,000 feet. One section of three Ju88s was a little way behind and I led 'Red Section' at it, and fastened on to the port aircraft and fired half my rounds at him from 200 yards. He then broke out of formation and headed off south-east in a slight dive with his port engine smoking. On being engaged from above I left him. I then climbed up and attacked a straggler in a beam attack, firing the remainder of my ammunition at 200 yards. His port engine caught fire and he also headed south-east. His port motor ticking over.

Along with Crossley's claims, Flying Officer John Humpherson destroyed a Junkers Ju88, which crashed five miles west of Chichester.

Landing back at Biggin, the pilots climbed from their cockpits gave their reports to the Intelligence officer, then slumped back into their Lloyd Loom chairs or lay on the grass with a cup of well-earned tea, hoping that would be the final flight of the day.

Sadly they would be disappointed, when at 6.50 pm; the scramble bell was rung again, and the men of 32 Squadron were ordered off to patrol over the aerodrome as reports of another enemy raid had filtered in. As they circled the aerodrome, the pilots could see in the distance that smoke was rising from the vicinity of Croydon aerodrome. The Germans had in fact mistaken Croydon as RAF Kenley through a navigational and visual error..

No. 32 Squadron headed for Croydon and on arriving found a formation of bomb-carrying Messerschmitt 109 and 110s of Erprobungs Gruppe 210 dive-bombing the drome. In conjunction with Hurricanes of No. 111 Squadron, who delivered a head-on attack against the Messerschmitts, claiming five of the enemy machines, the attack was driven off. A secondary target attack by Dorniers on the airfield at West Malling was also repelled by 32 Squadron, who claimed three Dornier 17s, two Ju88s and four 109s destroyed. Sergeant Leonard Pearce of 'B' Flight who destroyed one of the Dornier 17s reported.

I selected a Dornier 17 flying south from the Croydon district and when about 600 yards from it, I saw another Hurricane level with me. I dived and came up below it, firing into the front fuselage mainly. I fired 600 rounds in a five second burst from 300 yards closing to 75 yards; while the other Hurricane attacked from astern. The port engine caught fire and the enemy aircraft dived on fire at Redhill.

Sergeant Bernard Henson also claimed a Dornier 17 as probably destroyed, but he was attacked by a Messerschmitt fighter, his engine crankcase was pierced by bullets and he had to force-land at Tangmere aerodrome.

No. 610 Squadron had also been busy against the German fighter opposition. They had encountered 109s over Maidstone and had to deal with being at a disadvantage, when the German fighters came down from above. Pilot Officer Cox in his engagement with one of the 109s claimed he had probably destroyed it, while Sergeant Douglas Corfe damaged another fighter and attacked a bomber though he saw no results. Thankfully, no further raids took place that evening; it had been one of the toughest days yet against the Luftwaffe.

Both 32 and 610 Squadrons were heavily involved in actions on 16th August, when large raids were picked up by radar approaching the coast off Dover. 32 Squadron were scrambled at 12.15 pm, led by acting Squadron Leader Michael Crossley who had taken over command of the squadron from Squadron Leader John Worrall, who was given the role as Senior Sector Controller at the aerodrome. As the squadron climbed up they were given the position of the enemy by ground control, just as they neared Dover they sighted a formation of fifteen 109s. Crossley positioned his pilots to attack and dived down.

During this battle with the 109s, Crossley was able to destroy one of the enemy fighters which crashed into the sea two miles off Folkestone. Pilot Officer Peter Gardner claimed another as did Pilot Officer De Grunne. Later that afternoon, they were in action once more, when they received information of a large raid heading towards the Biggin Hill area. At 5.30 pm, the squadron encountered a formation of fifty-plus Junkers Ju88 twin engine bombers with a mixed escort of Messerschmitt 110s and 109s. Orders were given that they would attack the formation using a head-on attack. Michael Crossley gave a good account of what followed next:

> We attacked the main body almost head-on, which split them up. I then singled out a straggling formation of three 88s just behind and took the starboard one from in front and below, firing half my ammunition. It immediately caught fire and started to spin. This was seen by Pilot Officer John Pain in Blue Section. A moment later I opened fire from 250 yards, using the remainder of my bullets from behind at a Me110, who came across in front of me. After a fairly long burst of fire, his port engine caught ablaze and a stream of white smoke, possible petrol or coolant poured from his starboard engine. He went down steeply in a south-westerly direction.

Arriving back at Biggin, the following claims were reported to the squadrons' intelligence officer. Pilot Officer Richard Barton claimed two 109s probably destroyed, Pilot Officer John Pain, a Ju88 probably destroyed, Sergeant Leonard Pearce, a 109 destroyed over Heathfield, Flight Lieutenant Peter Brothers, a Ju88 which crashed into the sea about twelve miles south of Brighton. Sergeant E.A. Bayley damaged a 109, Michael Crossley with a Ju88 destroyed and a Me110 probably destroyed. The squadron had given a good account of itself that day.

610 Squadron took off from Hawkinge at 4.15 pm, to intercept a raid over Dungeness, where they were confronted with a large formation of fifty Junkers Ju88s and twelve Messerschmitt 109s flying at 25,000 feet. John Ellis put his squadron in the most favourable position to attack and battle commenced. Ellis attacked a Ju88 and saw it emitting smoke from one of the engines. Sergeant Stanley Arnfield fired at one of the escorts and saw his bullets enter into the cockpit area, while Pilot Officer Donald Gray fired at a 109 and saw it turn over and dive with its engine smoking. On their return to base, they claimed one 109 destroyed, one Ju88 and 109 damaged. Sadly they suffered one casualty, that of Acting Flight Lieutenant William Warner who failed to return in Spitfire R6802; he was subsequently listed as 'missing in action.'

During these combats, a number of German aircraft had crashed in the local vicinity, and two enemy pilots who had survived their ordeal had been captured and were being held under guard at Biggin Hill, before they were taken away for interrogation and then to be sent to a prisoner of war camp. Peter Brothers and some of the other officers of 32 Squadron found out and decided to invite one of the German captives over to their dispersal as a guest

> I remember that there was a German pilot whom we had shot down and he had landed near to Biggin and was picked up and put in the guard room, pending collection. When we had finished, flying we had him sent over under guard to the officers' mess for a drink. He said 'that the Luftwaffe would blacken the skies with their aircraft for the next few days and totally eliminate the RAF.' We actually had him out on our dispersal before we took him to the mess, because we were still on duty.
>
> We walked him over to our dispersal hut and we had to keep a very close watch on our three Polish pilots, because we thought they might have a go at him. We had a wing of a 109 propped up against the hut wall, we told him it was a wing from one of his aircraft and all he would say was 'maybe,' he wasn't going to give anything away information wise.
>
> The Poles just sat in the corner glowering at him; they couldn't understand us giving him a good time. I could understand their viewpoint, their country had been overrun, and they didn't know whether their families were still alive. They were naturally very tough indeed and they didn't give a damn if they were killed or not. All they wanted to do was kill as many Germans as they could.

On 18th August 1940, the Luftwaffe continued its attacks against the major RAF airfields in the south-east. The main targets for that day were to be Biggin Hill, Hornchurch, Kenley and North Weald. The Germans had hoped to launch their first raids during that morning, but weather conditions on the French side of the Channel were not satisfactory; so they postponed the attacks until mid-morning. A letter written by a German airman Feldwebel Wanderer tells of his memories of the day's attack, from the opponents viewpoint:

> 'Get Up' the first words of the day shook me out of my slumber. A look at the weather was the first thing. Clear Skies today? Clothes on, and a gulp of hot coffee, and then off to the truck which brings us to the aircraft. There I was in for a major disappointment, when the squadron leader announced that the target 'Biggin Hill' had been postponed as the weather was not ideal. So it meant waiting till midday then suddenly it was all go. The control tower gave the all clear for take-off and the whole squadron was roaring across the airfield. Once airborne we circled the airfield, then set course for England. The other squadrons joined us during the approach, a magnificent sight, the whole of the bomber wing consisting of about 50 planes. The pilots command 'assemble machine guns' reminded me that it was for real this time. I checked the two machine guns twice to make sure. Our fighter escort approached us as we neared the French coast. Now the sky was full of black dots to the left and right of us. The altimeter told us that we needed to put on our oxygen masks. Very soon the white strip of coast was visible beneath us, the English coast.
>
> We now expected anti-aircraft fire, but not a shot was fired and we continued towards our target unchallenged. 'Drop bombs' was announced, the heavy parcels were raining down. There will be nothing left intact down there? A turn to the left and the target became visible. A huge cloud of black smoke told us that the bombs had hit home. A single anti-aircraft gun made its presence known, but we were nowhere near. No English fighters, no anti-aircraft came anywhere near us. Where are the English, we kept asking ourselves. There was no sign of them at all and we headed for home unchallenged. Soon we were again over the French coast and we dropped altitude and did not need our oxygen masks anymore. No one in the squadron had ever experienced such a quiet run during a mission. Was this the end of Tommy?

British radar began to pick up signals of Luftwaffe formations beginning to form over the French coast at 12.30 pm. A large plot of 300 aircraft was heading towards the south-east, heading for Hornchurch, 60 Heinkels of I/KG1 headed for Biggin Hill. Fighter Command headquarters immediately gave out the order to all fighter stations to get their aircraft scrambled to meet the threat. At 12.55 pm, Biggin Hill control ordered 32 Squadron to get airborne and a few minutes later Spitfires of 610 Squadron received the same instructions. Once strapped into their cockpits the pilots hurriedly taxied down the runway and got into the air.

Once airborne both squadrons received instructions that their targets were nearing the area of Tunbridge Wells. RAF Kenley had been hit first, when a formation of nine Dornier 17s from 9/KG 76 came in undetected at low-level and dropped their bombs, which plastered the flightpaths causing large craters, destroying the operations room and two of the aerodrome three hangars. Following the raid on Kenley, the aerodrome at Croydon was hit as was West Malling. The enemy formation then turned its attentions to Biggin Hill. As they headed towards Biggin, the German formation which consisted of around sixty bombers with an escort of forty Messerschmitt 109s and 110s were met by the Hurricanes of 32 Squadron led by Michael Crossley. He decided that the only tactic he could employ to break up this formidable formation was to deliver a head-on attack. He positioned the squadron and went into the attack. His combat report tells what happened next:

> We carried out the head-on attack on the main formation of Dornier 215s. I climbed and saw a single Junkers Ju 88 about 2,000 feet below. I did a quarter attack on it, and after about five seconds there appeared to be an internal explosion, which injured the flight engineer, and masses of bits flew off all around. I pulled up sharply to avoid them and flew alongside to observe the results, including damage to the right engine. He jettisoned his bombs and his undercarriage came down and he glided down and crashed near Ashford at Romney Marsh.

> While carrying out the head-on attack, I took the starboard machine and Red 3 (Flying Officer Barton) said that it turned sharply up out of line, but could not confirm that it had crashed.
>
> I carried out another head-on attack on a Messerschmitt 110 and caused its port engine to issue a stream of white smoke, but owing to my attention being taken elsewhere, I did not follow it up.

610 Squadron which had mustered fifteen Spitfires into the air, engaged a force of fifty enemy bombers with an equal amount of fighters five-miles east of Biggin Hill. 'B' Flight was given the job of going after the Messerschmitts, while 'A' Flight went for the bombers. They succeeded in claiming three Dornier 215s, a Dornier 17, one Heinkel 111 and a Messerschmitt 110. 'B' flight had similar success in destroying five 109s.

Their casualties consisted of two damaged Spitfires R6694 flown by Pilot Officer Constantine Pegge, his aircraft received battle damage from a 109 and on landing caused further damage when hitting a bomb crater; the other R6993 piloted by Flight Lieutenant John Ellis whose Spitfire had been hit by cross-fire from the Heinkel bombers he had been attacking.

Despite the actions of the two squadrons, the German bombers still managed to press on and deliver their attack on Biggin Hill. At 1.30 pm, a formation of Heinkels arrived over the aerodrome and unloaded their deadly cargo. A number of the aerodrome's buildings were hit including the motor transport sheds, as were a substantial area along the flightpaths and runways. One of the aerodrome's Bofors gun emplacements also was hit, killing one of the gunners and injuring the rest of the crew. The raid last several minutes and once finished the personnel emerged from their shelters to survey the damage and assist any casualties. Around 500 bombs had been dropped on the aerodrome of which ninety had been time-delay action bombs. Apart from the bombs that had exploded on the flightpaths, many of the unexploded ones also littered the area.

An act of bravery now took place; when a WAAF named Sergeant Joan Eugene 'Elizabeth' Mortimer who had been a telephonist in the station armoury and had continued to relay messages throughout the raid.

Now observing the state of the flightpaths with craters and unexploded ordnance, and knowing that the squadrons would soon have to land and refuel and re-arm; she grabbed an armful of red marker flags on poles and went out onto the field and began to mark the unexploded ones. One of the bombs did explode nearby to her, knocking her off her feet, but she picked herself up and continued her job. In the meantime, other personnel did their best to clear up the debris and fill in the craters. Sergeant Mortimer was later recommended for an award for her courage and devotion to duty that day. On 5th November, she received the Military Medal.

Three of 32 Squadrons pilots were shot down during this action; Pilot Officer John Pain in Hurricane P3147 was hit by enemy fire and his aircraft caught alight during combat over Biggin at 1.45 pm, he abandoned the aircraft over Brenchley and landed slightly wounded at Horsmonden. He was admitted to the hospital in Tunbridge Wells. The second casualty was Sergeant Bernard Henson flying V6536 his aircraft received bullets in the gravity tank and he was obliged to carry out a forced-landing at Otford. He suffered a slight wound to the face, but apart from this was flying the next day. His Hurricane was damaged, but repairable.

While in combat over the aerodrome Flight Lieutenant Humphrey a' Beckett Russell's aircraft V7363 was hit by a 20mm cannon shell from a Messerschmitt 109, which exploded in the cockpit. Russell received wounds to his elbow, but more seriously was the wound to his left leg, which was pouring blood profusely. He quickly vacated his aircraft and pulled his parachute ripcord and slowly floated down, but more urgent was the loss of blood from his leg. As he came down, he managed to stem the flow of blood by using a cord from his oxygen mask and using it as a tourniquet. Once landing, he was quickly taken to Edenbridge Hospital, where the doctors worked on his leg. He would later return to the squadron and take over as its commander. His Hurricane crashed south of Lingfield Road at Skeynes Park.

On the lighter side, Roger Frankland working as a controller in the Ops Room remembers the first attack on the airfield:

> Just before we were bombed, we had a look-out on top of the officers' mess, so we could have a visual on anything. I asked him to tell me what sort of aircraft they were and his reply came to me 'I don't rightly know Sir' but I am being attacked by a swarm of bees.' I can't think of anything wittier than that about the Battle of Britain, it certainly stuck in my mind.

Aircraftsman Albert Hargraves served as a Bowser driver on the aerodrome:

> It was my birthday on the day the raids against Biggin Hill began. The Germans came in with the sun at the back of them. They came over bombing and strafing. Four of my pals in the motor transport section were going to go out with me for a drink that evening to celebrate my birthday. I never saw them again, they were killed. The celebration was cancelled.

One of the German bombers that had been involved in the raid against RAF Kenley, a Dornier 17Z-2 of KG76, was actually brought down close to Biggin Hill and crashed into a field at Leaves Green and burnt out at 1.30 pm. The crew consisting of Hauptmann Joachim Roth, Hauptmann Gustav Peters, Oberleutnant Rudolf Lamberty, Oberfeldwebel Valentin Geier and Feldwebel Hugo Eberhart all survived and were made prisoners of war.

The shooting down of this Dornier, although not directly attributed to any of the Biggin Hill Squadrons, has always been of fascination to those interested in the Battle of Britain. Firstly, there was controversy of who shot it down? Was it the ground defences or fighter aircraft. It was quickly ruled out that although the aircraft had been shot at by members of the 4th Platoon of the Kent Home Guard, who had fired off over one hundred rounds as it passed low overhead, it was actually brought down by Sergeant William Dymond of No. 111 Squadron.
But also flying that day was Flight Lieutenant Stanley Dudley Pierce

Connors, who had been with the squadron since 1938, he was an extremely experienced fighter pilot having fought over France and Dunkirk, being awarded the Distinguished Flying Cross at the end of May for his bravery in destroying a number of enemy aircraft. During the attack by the Dorniers against Kenley, witnesses claimed to have seen the bombers coming over the airfield followed behind by a single-seat fighter; this was at first thought to have been a Messerschmitt 109, but as the Dorniers had no fighter escort, it must have been a Hurricane chasing them; this could have been Stanley Connors? No. 111 Squadron based at Croydon had been scrambled immediately as the German formation entered the Godstone area, having already been sighted by the Observer Corps.

The squadron headed for Kenley where they sighted the low-flying Dorniers who had just pounded the aerodrome; the air was full of anti-aircraft fire and one of the Dorniers had been brought down by a parachute cable. Connors Hurricane was seen to follow the Dorniers through this maelstrom and latch onto one of the German aircraft as it turned away from Kenley trying to make its escape back to France. This aircraft was flown by Rudolf Lamberty.

At Layhams Farm, close to Biggin Hill, a Local Defence Volunteer Unit were suddenly aware of aircraft engines and the sound of gunfire heading their way, one of the volunteers who witnessed the commotion later recalled that as he looked south along the valley, which runs below the level of Biggin Hill, he saw a twin-engine aircraft flying very low with its wing burning and smoke trailing and behind this was a Hawker Hurricane, which to was emitting black smoke and flames coming from underneath the nose section. He also witnessed another twin-engine bomber who was following behind the Hurricane. Suddenly the Hurricane fell from the sky in flames and crashed into the ground. The aircraft had come down in an orchard. This was Stanley Connors Hurricane.

Two of the LDV wanted to race down to the burning Hurricane and see if they could save the pilot, but their commanding officer gave orders for them to stay back as the belts of ammunition exploded, making them wait until the fire had died down. After about fifteen minutes, the officer told the two volunteers to go down and guard the remains of the Hurricane. On arriving at the scene, they observed that the aircraft's Rolls Royce Merlin engine had come away from its mounting and lay further up the hill; most of the airframe had burnt. The body of the unfortunate pilot lay clear of the main wreckage; he had been thrown clear, but was badly burned.

They stood guard for about two hours until a RAF Crossley ambulance arrived and a corporal stepped out to retrieve the body. He was helped by the two young volunteers to wrap the pilot's body in a blanket and then placed it on a stretcher. The RAF corporal then asked one of the men if he had a knife, which he did, then the corporal cut the pilot's identity disc string, and then he dropped the two discs into the young man's hand, which read P/O S.D.P. Connors.

Other pilots from 111 Squadron had attacked the Dorniers that day. The squadron operations book states:

> Sergeant Ron Brown led Blue Section down to attack and destroy one Dornier and damage another two seriously. Yellow Section led by Sergeant Dymond followed in line astern and destroyed a further Dornier (Lamberty's) which crashed near Biggin Hill; two of its occupants were seen to shelter near a wood. Flight Lieutenant Connors DFC fell in flames and was killed. Yellow 1 gave the position of the crash from the air on his return and said that ack-ack fire from the hill could have caused the crash.

Rudolf Lamberty's Dornier had continued its course, but every second the pilot battled to keep the doomed aircraft in the air, he knew he would have to crash-land eventually. Two of the crew, Peters and Geier decided to bale-out, but they were at extremely low height, their parachutes did not fully deploy and both suffered multiple injuries. The third crewman, Eberhart struggled to the escape hatch, deployed his parachute before jumping, thus giving him the extra seconds needed to parachute safely down.

Lamberty and his navigator Roth stayed with the aircraft as he brought it down and crash-landed into a field at Leaves Green. As it came to a shuddering halt, both men desperately opened the escape hatch and clambered out, both injured, Roth was badly burned. As they retreated from the burning wreck they were soon confronted by a group of Home Guard volunteers with rifles pointed in their direction. Once all of the crew were collected, they were taken to the sick quarters at Biggin Hill aerodrome, where they were treated for their injuries and burns.

For many years a number of publications have listed that Stanley Connors aircraft crashed at 'The Oaks' Wallington, when in fact it came down approximately about half a mile directly behind Lamberty's Dornier. His Hurricane R4187 was in a field adjacent to Blackness Lane near Keston Church.

However, the day was far from over in regards to the Luftwaffes raids and at around 5.00 pm, another raid was picked up crossing the French coast consisting of 250 aircraft belonging to Luftflotte 2 who were based at various airfields north of the River Seine including Lille, Cambrai and Montididier. Their targets this time was Hornchurch and North Weald and fortunately not Biggin. At 5.30 pm, 32 Squadron was scrambled along with 501 Squadron based at Gravesend to intercept a formation heading for Hornchurch.

At 5.45, they sighted the formation at an altitude of 12,000 feet coming in north of Herne Bay. As 32 prepared to intercept, they were suddenly bounced in a surprise attack by Messerschmitts of II/JG51. During this attack, the Hurricane of Pilot Officer De Grunne V6535 was hit and burst into flames; he managed to bale-out suffering from burns and wounds and on landing was quickly taken to Willesborough Hospital to receive urgent treatment. This was his last flight with the squadron and did not return. Another casualty was Sergeant Leonard Pearce in Hurricane R4106 whose aircraft was also badly damaged enough to cause him to take to his parachute near Canterbury. He too was slightly wounded and did not return to the squadron, but on recovery was posted to 249 Squadron that September. His aircraft crashed at Rose Garden Cottage, Chartham Hatch.

After the initial attack by the 109s, the squadron was able to engage and do battle with the enemy, shooting down a number of 109s and 110s and a Dornier 215.

Michael Crossley was on his way back to the aerodrome, when he sighted a formation of Messerschmitt 110s flying in line astern. He decided that he would have a go at them, but as a result his Hurricane was hit badly by return machine gun fire and he was forced to abandon his aircraft, baling-out over Gillingham. He slowly floated down landing in an allotment field at Speaks Bottom, south of Gillingham being met by members of the local Home Guard, who took him for a drink at the Queen's Arms pub. His Hurricane N2461 crashed into the ground at Lidsing near Bredhurst.

A number of enemy aircraft were claimed by the other pilots of 32 Squadron including Pilot Officer Wlasnowolski who on landing back at Biggin Hill unfortunately taxied into a bomb crater.

The next following days were very quiet, due to the detrition of the weather, being cloudy with heavy rain showers, the Luftwaffe only sending over a few reconnaissance aircraft.

On 20th August, news was received at 32 Squadron that four of their pilots were to receive awards. Acting Squadron Leader Michael Crossley was awarded the Distinguished Service Order, while Flying Officers Rupert Smythe and John Humpherson and Peter Gardner would each receive the Distinguished Flying Cross. No doubt a few pints were downed in celebration that evening in the officers' mess.

The Luftwaffe resumed its attacks on Thursday 22nd August, although the weather was far from perfect, when raids were launched against shipping and the port of Dover, as well as targeting Manston aerodrome. Both 32 and 610 Squadrons saw action, first was 32 who during a patrol over Dover, met the enemy and both Flight Lieutenant Brothers and Pilot Officer Wlasnowolski shared in bringing down a 109 over Folkestone.

No.610 patrolled Folkestone at 1.00 pm at 15,000 feet, when they were attacked from above and out of the sun by twenty 109s, which dived through the Spitfires and back into cloud. Sergeant Corfe's aircraft was hit by cannon fire and he was forced to crash-land near Hawkinge aerodrome, he escaped injury, but the Spitfire caught alight and burnt out.

The next day 32 Squadron again was scrambled, Pilot Officer Jan Pfeiffer was the only pilot to engage the enemy, but received battle damaged to his aircraft, which crashed on landing at Hawkinge with only one wheel operating in Hurricane P2795, he was taken to the Kent and Canterbury Hospital suffering from severe shock and slight injuries, the aircraft was repairable.

During the afternoon, 610 Squadron were on patrol at an altitude of 15,000 feet over Folkestone, when they came under a surprise attack as twenty Messerschmitt's dived out of the sun and tore through the unsuspecting Spitfires. Four of the Spitfires were damaged during the attack, but managed to get back to base, only Spitfire R6695 flown by Sergeant Douglas Corfe was severely damaged and burst into flames causing him to extricate himself quickly as the aircraft became engulfed and crashed as an inferno at Hawkinge. Corfe landed unhurt.

During the early morning of 24th, all four sections of 610 Squadron were rapidly scrambled at 7.58 am as three large enemy formations were picked up off the south-east coast. The first to spot these was Sergeant Ronald Hamlyn who reported that the enemy aircraft were stepped up in line astern at 12,000 feet off Ramsgate. They went into the attack and Hamlyn destroyed a Junkers Ju88, watching it dive into the sea, he then attacked a 109 fighter and this he also sent into the sea on fire.

The remainder of the squadron split up and did not engage. Sergeant Arnfield suffered damage to his aircraft and was forced to take to his chute. On landing he unfortunately fractured his left ankle and was admitted to the Victoria Hospital at Deal. His Spitfire R6686 fell to earth in flames at Hammill, near Eastry.

They were again called upon at 10.35 am and asked to patrol over Hawkinge and then Gravesend and finally Dover, and it was here that they encountered six Messerschmitt 109s. During this combat Flying Officer Peter Lamb and Sergeant Ron Hamlyn both destroyed an enemy fighter, one crashing into the sea off Cap Gris Nez and the other crashing in flames three miles inland near Calais, while Flying Officer Eric Aldous claimed a probable. Pilot Officer Gray was wounded during the encounter and was obliged to force-land Spitfire X4102 at Shepherdswell, he was taken to the local hospital at Waldershire for treatment.

Their final sortie of the day took place over Gravesend during the afternoon, when Blue, Red and Yellow Sections intercepted twenty Junkers Ju88s and twenty 109s at 15,000 feet at 3.45 pm; the squadron engaged this formation north of the Isle of Sheppey and were again successful in destroying four enemy fighters and one probably destroyed. Two of these were claimed by Sergeant Ronald Fairfax Hamlyn, whose score for that day had risen to five; the only RAF fighter pilot to claim so many in a single day. Hamlyn who came from Harrogate, had joined the RAF for pilot training in 1936 and on the outbreak of war, he joined his first squadron, No. 72 at Church Fenton. On 6th June 1940, he was sent on detachment to 610 Squadron at Gravesend and this became a full posting. Hamlyn was later awarded the Distinguished Flying Medal the following month on 13th September 1940

Flight Lieutenant Stanley Norris and Sergeant Aubrey Baker each claimed a 109 from this action with Pilot Officer Constantine Pegge, a probable. Pilot Officer Claude Merrick suffered a slight wound and crashed his Spitfire L1037 at Fyfield, near Ongar in Essex, where he received treatment at the local hospital. It had been an extremely busy day for 610.

No. 32 Squadron flew four operational sorties that day, the first at 2.30 pm, when they were scrambled to intercept a raid heading for Hornchurch, coming in over Dover. As they approached a formation of Heinkels, they were bounced by 109s. No claims were made and no casualties were sustained during this encounter, they landed back at base 90 minutes later. But at 3.45, they were ordered up again to patrol over Hawkinge where they met fifteen 109s coming in over Folkestone.

This time they had better success, claiming three destroyed, one each for Flight Lieutenant Peter Brothers, Pilot Officer Keith Gillman and Sergeant William Higgins, Pilot Officer Karol Pniak claimed a probably destroyed; while Pilot Officer Anthony Barton damaged another as did Sergeant Donald Aslin. Not so lucky was Rupert Smythe whose Hurricane V6568 was badly hit by enemy return fire and he had to crash-land at Lyminge wounded. He was taken to the Royal Masonic Hospital at Hammersmith in London to undergo surgery for his injuries.

Pilot Officer Eugene Seghers, a Belgian, was also shot down, but was able to bale-out and landed in the sea and was picked up by a rescue boat. His Hurricane V6567 crashed at Tedders Leas near Eltham. Karol Pniak's Hurricane V6572 was also hit and he too was forced to vacate his aircraft. He sustained knee and ankle injuries due to a heavy landing and was admitted to hospital. The Hurricane crashed to earth at Rhodes Minnis near Lyminge.

Squadron Leader Mike Crossley had to make a crash-landing with his undercarriage in the up position after receiving battle damage from a 109 fighter. He tightened the straps on his Sutton harness and prepared for the landing. His Hurricane P3481 skidded across a field at Valley Farm, Lyminge and came to a grinding halt at 4.30 pm; he stepped out from his cockpit uninjured, but the aircraft was a write-off. No. 32 Squadron flew two more sorties that day, but these were to prove uneventful. Peter Brothers combat report of the second patrol that day details his claim of the Messerschmitt he destroyed:

> I was leading Blue Section at 15.00 hours on 24/8/40, when we were attacked by about 12 Me109s which had been circling above us for some time. As we climbed up to them they climbed away and kept their distance until an opportune moment, when they dived on us. I fired short bursts at two or three and then lost them owing to 'blacking out'. But I climbed up to 20,000 feet and engaged them again and managing to get on the tail of one, I gave him two 3-second bursts. Part of his starboard wing came away and he dived into the sea about 10-miles south-east of Dover. I followed him down, then returned to base

'B' Flight of 32 Squadron led by Flight Lieutenant Brothers was sent off from their forward base at Hawkinge on 25th August after an enemy formation was picked up heading towards Dover, but they were ordered back when the enemy formation turned back. There was no further action until early evening at 7.00 pm, when both 32 and 610 were ordered to scramble. 32's Hurricanes were able to engage with twelve Dornier 215s before they too were attacked by the bombers escorting fighters numbering at least thirty-six 109s. Mike Crossley claiming a Dornier and a Me109 destroyed, Pilot Officer Jack Rose damaged a Dornier before he himself came under attack and was shot down by a 109. Pilot Officer Hector Proctor also destroyed a further 109, which crashed in flames four miles east of Cap Gris Nez. Pilot Officer Barton sighted a Henschel He126 reconnaissance aircraft near Dungeness and attacked it as it reached mid-channel and sent it into the sea.

Jack Rose who had joined the squadron on 22nd August, had previously served with No. 3 Squadron in France during May. That morning before the squadron had been scrambled; each of the pilots had been issued with a packet of fluorescence dye to stitch into their life jackets or Mae Wests as they were commonly known. This was used if a pilot had to parachute into the sea; the greenish-yellow dye would then react with the water and leave a stain clearly visible from the air showing the downed pilots position, so he could be rescued. Rose decided he would stich his dye packet on, while others didn't. During the engagement he was shot down in Hurricane V6547 and was forced to bale-out over the sea, as he would later recall:

> I was flying as No. 2 of Red Section when I attacked a Dornier and fired a burst from my guns down its fuselage from astern and my second burst fired at the port engine. Its engine began smoking when I was myself attacked by a Me109. My rudder controls were shot away and I escaped by parachute and was eventually picked up by a speed boat.

After, landing in the water, he was floating for two hours, during which time he must have nearly given up any hope of being rescued. Fortunately an aircraft from his own squadron which had been searching for him spotted the coloured stain in the water and a rescue craft was directed to him and he was picked up.

32 Squadron's only fatality was that of Pilot Officer Keith Gillman who was shot down into the Channel off Dover. His body was never found and his name is remembered on the Runnymede Memorial Panel 8.

610 Squadron in the meantime had run into the Messerschmitt 109 escort, which had been flying 5, 000 feet higher than themselves. The squadron climbed up to attack and Sergeant Bob Beardsley opened fire from 300-yards, his bullets entering the cockpit of one of the German aircraft, causing it to flick on to its back and go into a vertical dive. Pilot Officer Lamb was able to confirm seeing the enemy crash.

Pilot Officer Frederick Gardiner was wounded and baled out landing near Sandwich, after which he was admitted to Waldershire Hospital, Shepherdswell near Dover. His Spitfire K9931 crashed and burnt out at Stoneheap Farm near Northbourne. Sergeant Parsons had sighted a green dye streak in the water, about five miles off Dover. He circled around until a rescue launch picked up a pilot. It was not known whether this was an RAF or Luftwaffe pilot?

On 26th August, just after midday, 610 Squadrons Spitfires had been scrambled and intercepted a small formation of Messerschmitt 109s over Dover. They managed to claim one of the enemy fighters destroyed and another as probably destroyed. Following this encounter, they were vectored on to another formation of Dornier 215 bombers with a fighter escort and managed to destroy a bomber.

During this attack, Flying Officer Frank Webster's Spitfire R6595 had been badly damaged during combat with one of the 109 escort fighters over Folkestone; and while attempting to land at Hawkinge, his aircraft stalled and crashed and exploded in flames at Drellingore, just north-east of the aerodrome, killing Webster. His remains were taken back to his home town of Sandown on the Isle of Wight.

Sergeant Peter Else was the squadrons other casualty from that sortie, he too had received attention from the enemy fighters. His aircraft

P9496 had been hit from astern and set alight. Else had tried to bale-out, but as he unlocked the cockpit door in preparation to vacate his Spitfire, the enemy fighter fired another burst from his guns, which hit Else in his left forearm and shattered it. He managed withstanding the terrible pain to get out of his aircraft at 20,000 feet and floated down and landed fortunately on Hawkinge aerodrome.

He was quickly attended and taken to the Kent County Hospital at Canterbury, where they found that the injuries to his left arm were to severe, so they had to amputate, just below the elbow. He last remembered seeing his left hand still attached to the control column. He also received treatment to burns on his face and right hand. He was discharged from the RAF on medical grounds in April 1941, but was given work as an aircraft inspector at No. 22 Elementary Flying Training School at Marshall's aerodrome in Cambridgeshire.

Sergeant Pilot Cyril Bamberger of 610 Squadron who in July had been sent by his commanding officer to No. 7 OTU, Hawarden to gain further experience on Spitfires, now returned to fly operationally with the squadron. He remembers his first day back at Biggin:

> I re-joined 610 Squadron on August 28th, many of the auxiliary pilots I had known pre-war had already been shot down and killed or injured and not many of the old pilots were left. The CO I had known as a pilot officer of the regular air force, but the squadron had already lost two commanding officers before I joined it and their morale was not particularly high.
>
> I went down to the dispersal hut and prepared to take on the German Air Force, but the squadron had landed at another airfield to re-arm and refuel. The air-raid siren sounded and there was one spare Spitfire, so I was scrambled just on my own for airfield defence and that was my first flight.
>
> I took off and climbed to about 15,000 feet, as the enemy plots were coming in to Biggin Hill. I couldn't see the bigger picture; all I could see was the aerodrome below and the controller telling me that enemy bombers were coming in. I was on my own and I was

no longer the confident aviator.

The adrenalin was flowing, but I didn't have the slightest idea what to expect or do. Fortunately the enemy raid was diverted to some other airfield and I was told to land. That was my first operational flight of which I did not see or shoot at the enemy.

On that same day, I then flew to Hawkinge which was the forward base and then I flew with the squadron on four patrols, from Hawkinge to Dungeness at 25,000 feet, hoping that a raid would come in. During the afternoon patrol at around 4.00 pm between Dover and Deal, we encountered a formation of about fifteen to twenty Messerschmitt 109s at 18,000 feet. I was flying in the position of Green 3 when we sighted the German aircraft above and travelling towards us.

We attacked and I managed to get on to the tail of one of the 109s and opened fire from 250 yards. After my third burst, the German turned over on to his back and black smoke began to bellow from his engine. I was not in the position to see if he crashed, as I was then engaged by another of his comrades and was forced to break away. On my return to base I claimed it as probably destroyed.

Flying from Hawkinge, you flew down there early morning from Biggin, and returned in the evening. You were nearer the enemy, but it wasn't a great advantage, I don't think it saved much fuel. I suppose in some ways we broke up attacks before they were allowed to get further inland. But we never were able to get the height and get above them as they were already at an advantage coming in. I remember that on a number of occasions that we were targeted by the big German guns at Calais who shelled Dover and Hawkinge.

I remember later, three of us were instructed to escort an Avro Anson twin-engine aircraft across the Channel, which I think was trying to locate and take photographs of these big German guns. It was the most stupid idea, who thought it up I have no idea.

We took off and the Anson climbed to about 2,000 feet, I don't know how far we got, about three quarters of the way, when as we expected we were suddenly approached by a number of Messerschmitt 109s. The Anson immediately turned for home and obviously we were there to protect it, which was asking the impossible. We buzzed around its tail, but the only thing we could do, was stop being shot down ourselves. I went right down to sea-level knowing that if a 109 wanted to get me, he would have to risk flying into the sea. All three of us got back, but one person in the Anson was killed, when it crash-landed.

Biggin Hill did receive further attention from the Luftwaffe on 27th August, fortunately most of the ordinance did not explode, but left a number of craters and holes with unexploded bombs across the flightpaths. Craters were hastily filled in by ground personnel, while the call went out for a bomb disposal team to come and start the procedure of defusing the bombs.

Most of the German bombs had been of the normal detonation type, but two of them were found to be 250 kilo-gram delayed-action. This called for a specialist technical officer from the UXB to come and look at them. At 6.00 pm, the Air Ministry contacted Squadron Leader Eric Moxey, the technical intelligence officer of the RAF Bomb Disposal and asked him if he could travel down to Biggin Hill and inspect the two bombs and remove the fuses.

On his arrival at the aerodrome, with his aide Warrant Officer E.G. Hunt, they were taken over to where the devices were laying and decided to try and defuse one of them. The area were they worked had been evacuated of all personnel and a silence fell over the aerodrome. Moxey was able to remove safely one of the fuses, but while trying for the second it went off, killing Moxey instantly and throwing his assistant over 30-feet away. Miraculously, Hunt survived the explosion.

The force of the explosion left little of the squadron leaders' body to identify, only remnants of his uniform and fragments of a diary. Group Captain Grice immediately telephoned the Air Ministry with the grim news. It was later recommended that Eric Moxey should receive a posthumous awarded for his gallant sacrifice in trying to make the bombs safe. In December 1940, his family received the posthumous George Cross Medal in his honour.

On this day No. 32 Squadron received orders to go north to Acklington for a rest period, which they badly needed; No. 79 flew back down to replace them. In fact, No. 32 Squadron would not return to Biggin Hill again. They had been stationed at the aerodrome for nine years and their leaving was summoned quite eloquently in their squadron diary, which read:

> Well, old Biggin Hill, 32 (F) Squadron bids you farewell. You brought us honour, excitement, fear, depression, happiness, tragedy, laughs, new associations, thrills – in short, every sentiment a man can experience in quick jumbled succession.
> Do we regret leaving you? Do the happiness and elation you brought us outweigh the sorrow and pain, and the indescribable 'eat, drink and be merry for tomorrow we die' sensation that each day brought? We don't know. We think perhaps not.
> No, we wouldn't have you again for worlds, but we would have missed you! You made men out of boys and we're grateful. So long Biggin Hill, 32 Squadron will never forget.

By the 28th August, No. 79 Squadron had returned from their rest period up at Acklington, some of their aircraft were ordered to the forward base at Hawkinge during the early morning. No sooner had 'B' Flight taken off from Biggin at 8.30 am when enemy aircraft were sighted just over the coast at 17,000 feet; a formation of thirty-three bombers escorted by Messerschmitt 109s of JG26, led by their commander Adolf Galland.

Other RAF fighters were also called into action including the Defiant Squadron of No. 264. They were no match for the 109s, who shot down three of the Defiants and damaged a further three with the loss of five aircrew killed. During this encounter Flight Lieutenant Clerke of 79 Squadron probably destroyed a Messerschmitt 109, while Pilot Officer

Nelson-Edwards claimed a Heinkel bomber as a probable.

Flight Lieutenant Haysom's aircraft P3938 was hit by a bullet in the Glycol system, causing him to make a force-landing at Appledore Station near Tenterden, he landed successfully with wheels down. American born Pilot Officer Alexander Zatonski from Philadelphia, who had joined the squadron on 13th July at Acklington was not so lucky, his Hurricane P2718 was shot down north of Folkestone, near Hythe, claimed by Oberleutnant Fritz Losigkeit. Although he managed to parachute out from his blazing aircraft, he did not escape injury and on landing was treated for burns at the Hythe Small Arms School. His Hurricane fell to earth south-east of Stonehill, Sellindge, Kent.

After landing at Hawkinge, following their encounter, they were ordered off again at 11.00 am, this time to intercept two Heinkel He.59 Floatplanes which were being escorted by three Messerschmitt 110 twin-engine fighters. They were engaged and one of the floatplanes was shot down, whilst the other was seen to land on the water damaged.

610 Squadron had also been in action that day and suffered the loss of one of their pilots. During an engagement with Messerschmitt 109s over Dover, Pilot Officer Kenneth Cox in Spitfire P9511 was shot down at 5.00 pm and his aircraft fell from the sky and crashed into a house at Selling Minnis. It is not known whether he was dead before his aircraft hit the building.

Fourteen Spitfires of 610 Squadron were available to intercept an incoming raid at 3.30 pm on 29th. Taking off from Biggin Hill they engaged sixty Dorniers plus their escort approaching from the south flying at varying heights from 16,000 feet upwards, over Mayfield in Sussex. The Spitfires managed to break up the formations, claiming one Messerschmitt 110 destroyed two 110s and two Dorniers probably destroyed and three Dorniers damaged. Their only loss was that of Sergeant Edward Manton who was listed as missing at the time, but soon after his Spitfire R6629 with his body was found to have crashed at the Great Wigsell Estate, Hurst Green, Sussex. He was buried at Hawkhurst Cemetery, Kent.

They flew another patrol over Hawkinge at 6.00 pm and met with six 109s at 25,000 feet. Sergeant Bob Beardsley was able to despatch one of the fighters which went into a steep diving turn damaged, while Sergeant Aubrey Baker attacked another which was last seen smoking heavily, diving into the sea.

Biggin Hill suffered a number of raids over the period of the 30th/31st August and 1st September. The first raid, which took place at around 11.15 am on Friday 30th, was fortunately intercepted by the squadrons of No. 79 and 610, who managed to deter the German Heinkel bombers to drop their bomb loads short of the actual aerodrome; although some of the ordinance caused damage in the Biggin Hill and Keston villages. During this raid, two Messerschmitt 109s of II/JG54 collided in mid-air over Biggin Hill, one spun down at Fickleshole Farm, Warlingham at 11.55 am. The other dived into the ground at Layhams Farm, Addington; both the pilots Oberleutnant Hans Rath and Leutnant Rudolf Ziegler were fortunate to bale out, and were captured. One came down by parachute at Detillins Lane, Oxted, the other at Hurst Green, south of Oxted, Surrey. During this same action Pilot Officer Paul Mayhew claimed one of the Heinkel bombers destroyed as did Pilot Officer Owen Tracey and Pilot Officer Bill Millington who claimed an additional Heinkel He111 and a Messerschmitt 110 as damaged.

Pilot Officer E.D. 'Teddy' Morris flying as 'Blue 1' was seen to ram a Heinkel bomber of 10/KG1 over Reigate, which was heading to bomb Farnborough. Morris managed to parachute to safety, landing at Dorking uninjured; his aircraft P3203 crashing at Lodge Farm, South Holmwood, Brockham. The Heinkel, Werke No. 2720 fell to earth at Swires Farm, Capel, south of Dorking, Surrey with the loss of all crew.

Six aircraft from 79 Squadron took off again at 6.05 pm and observed the aerodrome being bombed for a second time, while they were doing their first circuit. The enemy formation was made up of Junkers Ju88s with an escort of 30 Messerschmitt 109s and 110s. During the raid, they managed to intercept and claim two enemy fighters, both 109s by Flight Lieutenant Geoffrey Haysom and Sergeant Henry Bolton. Pilot Officer Paul Mayhew's aircraft was damaged when his tail-plane rudder was shot up by cannon fire from one of the Messerschmitt's.

The bombers managed to drop many high-explosive bombs which severely damaged workshops, some barracks and hangars The motor transport shed and worse still, severed the electricity, water and gas mains. The telephone services were also rendered useless.

The casualties inflicted on the ground among the RAF personnel was particularly high when three air-raid shelters received hits, causing the death of 39 airmen and one woman in one shelter alone. This was Mary Cremin aged 24 years, who worked as a NAAFI girl. In another shelter, which was occupied by members of the WAAF, a bomb had exploded almost on top of the shelter; this had blown in the shelter walls causing the women to be buried under earth and concrete.

Fortunately, the women were eventually dug out of their entombment by rescuers; some were suffering from shock and slight injuries, a few which were more seriously injured were given Morphia injections, before being transported to local hospitals. Those that had been killed in the raid were taken to the mortuary at Biggin Hill; this was soon full to capacity and the remaining bodies had to be taken to a temporary mortuary set up at Brickyard Farm in Jail Lane. Aircraftsman Albert Hargraves remembers the raid:

> We'd just come out of the canteen, when the station commander announced over the Tannoy that everybody who wasn't essential should go to the shelters; but so many dashed for the shelters that not everybody could get in. I dashed back to my bowser to drive down to the dispersal, where there were some trees. I'd just got clear of the main camp to get to the perimeter, when the Dorniers came down the middle of the aerodrome. They looked like they were only fifty feet off the ground, though they must have been higher.
>
> The cab doors of the bowser had been taken off previously to allow us to get in and out quickly. I pulled up sharp, jumped out and ran like bloody hell to a nearby hedge and lay down. The bombs were exploding and you could hear the machine guns from the Dorniers and Messerschmitts. Then it went quiet; the main

> shelter, the one where not everybody could get in, had been hit. There was a hell of a crater there.
>
> We rushed over and tried to get the people out. There were a lot of casualties. There were heads lying around and arms sticking up out of the crater. We were digging away there until three in the morning. We got about forty bodies out and there were still some left. The next day, they got a group of miners to help dig the shelter out. After they thought they'd got out as many as they could, they bulldozed the area over.

The only WAAF to be killed that day was Corporal Edna Lena Button aged 39, a nursing orderly, who originated from Tasmania. The body of another woman was found later lying by a hedge, the victim of enemy machine gun fire; this was a young woman named 'Trixie' who also worked in the NAAFI. Squadron Leader Roger Frankland, the Sector Controller in the Operations Room remembers the raids:

> When the Luftwaffe attacked us and at other airfields like Kenley, and North Weald; the enemy aircraft that came in had been undetected by flying low-level from a direction we were not expecting; and they made a pretty good job on the airfield by destroying a lot of buildings including some of the hangars.
>
> One bomb came down just outside the Ops Room and this put paid to any further control as far as that afternoon was concerned. The casualties were two killed, one bomb fell well behind me and hit one of the out buildings next to the Ops Room and demolished that, but fortunately no one in Ops was injured. We were covered in dust and debris, we brushed ourselves down and tried to carry on.
>
> After we were bombed we had to move in to other quarters, which was a butchers' shop in the village. Operating from there was slightly original, we had minuscule control; we had a land line and we could talk to the squadrons and give them plots. The work carried out by the Post Office engineers was incredible in keeping

> the lines open, working 24-hours a day, to keep the information coming through to the sector airfields, while the Germans kept up the bombing. They did a marvellous job.

The following account was given by Felicity Hanbury, an Assistant Section WAAF Officer serving on the aerodrome when the raids occurred:

> It was a sunny morning and I was talking to my flight sergeant in the guard-room about the ordinary routine of the day, when the station broadcast ordered one of the squadrons to 'come to readiness.' I told her that I might as well stay where I was for the time being and then go with her to one of the airwomen's slit trenches nearby, should a raid occur. The minutes passed by, but there were no further announcements, so I started to walk towards my office in the station headquarters building?
>
> Biggin was a delightful station, surrounded by rolling hills and green fields broken by little woods of cedar and beeches. The gardens of the officers' mess looked neat and pretty and the ivy climbing up the outside walls made a perfect natural camouflage.
>
> As I approached and entered the headquarters, the sirens began to wail and we were then told to go to the trenches. These were long rectangular concrete vaults, half underground and covered with mounds of earth. A few seconds later we heard one of our squadrons get into the air, then another, finally the civilian air-raid warning could be heard in the surrounding area. I glanced up at the sky and caught a glimpse of one of our squadrons, it was a comforting sensation.
>
> We had hardly settled down, when the noise of the patrolling aircraft overhead changed from a constant buzz to the zoom and clatter of a dog-fight. Then things happened quickly. There was a terrifying head-splitting roar which grew louder and louder, completely drowning out the sound of the combat above. 'We are being dive-bombed' said someone who still had her voice.

Most of the others sat quietly with their arms folded, but in one corner I noticed a girl with eyes closed who seemed to be whispering to herself. I learned later that she had been reciting the Lord's Prayer. An instant later, just as it seemed as if the noise couldn't become any more deafening without the aircraft coming through the top of the trench, bombs began crashing all around us. One landed a few feet away from the entrance to the trench. Its hot blast of air bowled us over like nine-pins and a shower of stones and chunks of earth poured down the steps of the shelter. I remember thinking, 'I suppose this is how one feels during an earthquake.'

I was just beginning to feel my ears, eyes and limbs belonged to me again, when the whole terrible process started again. The terrific shuddering and deafening noise made me feel as if my body was falling to pieces.

Among others who were in our shelter was a fighter pilot who had been stationed at Biggin Hill previously. He had landed a few minutes before the raid to get some minor repair done to his aircraft before returning to his home base. To his disgust and fury at having to sit in the trench during the raid is something I shall never forget. He moaned 'bloody bad luck, that's what it is, why Jerry couldn't have at least waited until my crate was fixed? Here I am sitting like a ninny while my pals are up there having a go at him.'

Then there was a lull broken only by the sound of our aircraft returning to refuel and rearm. A few minutes later a messenger arrived saying a trench had been hit on the edge of the aerodrome. The Padre and another officer followed the airman to the scene of the disaster and I thought I had better go and see if the airwomen were alright in their trenches. All was now deathly silent. I climbed through debris and around craters back towards the WAAF guardroom. As I drew nearer there was a strong smell of escaping gas. The mains had been hit. Through the window somebody shouted to me, 'Put your cigarette out before you blow the place to bits.' I complied.

One bomb had fallen on the airwomen's trench near the guardroom, burying the women who were sheltering inside; I couldn't help thinking how lucky I had been not to wait to go into that trench when the station broadcast had given us the preliminary warning. Looking off to the right of the runway, I noticed one of the NAAFI girls being laid under a hedge. I started to go towards her, but was stopped by an airman who whispered, 'the poor girl is dead'. I asked how it had happened 'machine guns, I suppose' said the airmen, 'you had better come along now, there is important work to be done at the trench.'

The Station Warrant Officer called for volunteers, among them was the Officer's Mess gardener, a dear old man who used to bring us fruit from his garden in the village. They got to work quickly and as the civilian 'all clear' went, the trench was uncovered. We had prepared ourselves for an awful sight, half expecting to find most of the girls dead, but we were happily mistaken. One by one, the girls were dug out. Some were hardly recognisable because of the dirt and dust on their faces. Others were dazed, whilst others were badly cut and bruised, but all were alive save one.

Those who were unhurt were in excellent form. First they asked about the raid, then they wanted cigarettes and then they offered to help. The wounded were calm and exceptionally brave. My flight sergeant who had damaged her back, begged me not to stay with her as there might be someone who needed more help than she did.

I heard later from a WAAF Corporal who was in the trench at the time, that they all had been blown by the blast into a jumbled heap. If there was any danger of panic in the trench it was quickly removed by the extraordinary performance of the flight sergeant. When she couldn't sit up, she exclaimed good naturedly, 'my heavens, I have broken my back!' A few seconds later she noticed an unnatural feeling in her mouth, she shouted 'I have broken my false teeth too!' The girls couldn't help but smile as she drew the pieces of her plate from her mouth one by one.

A few days later, I attended a service funeral at the nearby cemetery for the airwoman that had been killed. Even then we were not left in peace, the Luftwaffe came again forcing the civilian mourners to take cover in the surrounding hedges while the Padre continued the burial service. After a while I returned to headquarters to report to the station commander and was told that the WAAF Officer's Mess could not be used as there was a delayed action bomb in the garden. I, along with two WAAF Cipher Officers went to pack up and collect some of our things as quickly as we could. That night we had to sleep in the station commander's house. After some food, we went over to the WAAF Cookhouse to see how things were going there.

The Airwomen's Mess was the only building which had not been damaged by the raid and I could see that we would have to do all the cooking for the station for a bit. On the way there, I saw something like a white pillow lying on the ground, and as I approached to pick it up a voice said out of the darkness 'I shouldn't touch that if I was you Miss; it's marking a delayed action bomb.' I thanked him very much and tried hard not to look as though I was walking any quicker than I had been previously. Eventually I arrived at the Cookhouse to find the airwomen cooking virtually in the dark, but to their eternal credit of the cooks, they produced some delicious smelling sausages and mash to an endless stream of men going past the service hatch.

Many of the service personnel quarters were severely damaged or completely destroyed; so parties were sent out to see if any of the local people would oblige in letting airmen or women billet in their homes for a short period. Many villagers did help, but some were completely offish, stating that because of the aerodrome their lives had been put in danger. One large house in Bromley Common named the 'Cedars' was requisitioned for the WAAFs to billet in, others were billeted in houses in the villages around the local vicinity.

On 31st August, the aerodrome came under attack once more, firstly at 8.30 am when the air-raid alert was sounded; but this was driven off by RAF Fighters. Pilot Officer George Nelson-Edwards flying with 79 Squadron was shot down on that early sortie; his Hurricane aircraft was P3103 coded NV-T. In 1991, he recalled the event:

> It was my first sortie of the day and we met and engaged a number of Messerschmitt 109s, I was suddenly hit in the glycol tank and possibly elsewhere by bullets from a 109. I noticed it had a yellow spinner as it flashed past me, while I was still on the climb. I was then at about 2,000 feet and had only reached 250 knots or thereabouts. I was a sitting duck. The temperature went off the clock and my engine seized and stopped. Luckily for me the Messerschmitt pilot must have lost me, because he didn't make another pass, by which time it was taking all my powers of concentration to work out how to cope with my situation. I found a space of ground and prepared to make a crash-landing in between some trees; on landing the aircraft skidded to a halt finally coming to rest only a few feet from a brick wall of a large family house.
>
> On impact, I struck my forehead on something very hard, probably the gun-sight and I was knocked unconscious for a few moments. I had severe bruising to the right eye. I remember a man came out of the house holding a large glass of brandy. What struck me more was the gentleman had a large parrot resting on one of his shoulders and there were droppings down his back.
>
> He helped me into the house and here I was allowed to have a bath and given breakfast. I was looked after until the RAF arrived two hours later to pick me up. My aircraft was being guarded all this time by a Special Constable, Mr William Withers of Oxted. I later found out that the gentleman who had taken me in was named Mr Strong, who was in fact of German heritage and his house was called 'The Grange' now the 'Limpsfield Grange School.
>
> I returned to Biggin Hill and immediately was taken to the

sick-quarters, where the medical officer looked me over and took me off flying for 48-hours. My right eye was by now completely closed. Apart from a few cuts and bruises, I was otherwise OK.

The aerodrome was the target again when a formation of Dorniers at 12,000 feet was sighted at midday. The enemy bombers emptied their load, which caused damage to a few buildings, but more concerning was the bombs that had exploded on the runways. They had caused the runway to be almost unusable, so much so that some of the aircraft of No. 72 'Basutoland' Squadron who had just flown down from Acklington to begin operations had to divert to Croydon aerodrome to land, as did 79 Squadron.

The Luftwaffe paid Biggin Hill one more visit that day at 6.00 pm, when ten Junkers Ju88s suddenly appeared from the north-east and battered the station once more; destroying eight valuable Spitfires, setting ablaze the station armoury and knocking out communications yet again. The Operations Room block was also hit, but suffered no casualties with only minor injuries as a result of flying glass.

Two WAAFs who worked on communications near the Operations Room, Sergeant Helen Turner and Corporal Elspeth Henderson stayed at their post during the raid trying to get signals out to RAF Headquarters at Uxbridge, but they eventually had to vacate their post due to the damage caused by a bomb which crashed through the roof of the tele-printer room and exploded.

Seven aircraft of 79 Squadron had taken off from the aerodrome at 5.45 pm, just before the raid and had been instructed to patrol over Biggin. They encountered the incoming enemy aircraft and were able to claim some of them; Pilot Officer Owen Tracy destroyed a Dornier 17 and a Dornier 215, Pilot Officer 'Dimsie' Stones claimed a Dornier destroyed and another probably destroyed. Flying Officer Edward Morris was wounded in the combat and crashed his Hurricane P3877 on landing. Robert Deacon Elliott, then a 26 year old pilot officer with No. 72 Squadron, remembers his first day on arrival at the aerodrome:

We came in to land at Biggin Hill and 610 Squadron were just about to take off and head north for a rest led by their commanding officer John Ellis, they wanted to get the hell out of it as fast as they could. They had taken a bit of a battering and needed to rest and get new pilots and machines. We arrived at about 3.30 pm and we were called to readiness at once and later that evening at 5.45 pm, there was a big raid on the aerodrome. I was on the ground at the time, and the bombs hit the Operations Block and the Station Armoury, at dispersal some of the aircraft were on fire hit by incendiaries. Our commanding officer at that time was Squadron Leader Tony Collins, he was shot down the following day and made a force-landing near Hawkhurst between some trees and a haystack, but he was ok. We managed to shoot down three of the enemy accounted for by Jack Steere and Ted Graham. The aerodrome was in a dreadful state.

Assistant Section Officer Felicity Hanbury:

At 8.30 a.m. the next morning, the alert went again and we were ordered once more to take cover, but nothing happened to us as the attack was driven off. I spent the day visiting the cookhouse and sick quarters, arranging billets to accommodate the airwomen who had become homeless, arranging transport and visiting the injured in hospital. While at the cookhouse, there was another raid and once more we heard the roar and zoom of dog fights and the sound of bombs coming nearer. We laughed and joked in the trench and soon it was over and everybody was back at work as though nothing had happened.

Later that afternoon, as I was returning to the aerodrome with another WAAF officer, when we were caught in another attack and our choices of action were few. There was no time to get to a trench, so we hurriedly put on our tin hats and ran into a nearby wood. The edge of the wood was near a crossroads and as we ducked under the trees, a police bell-shelter opened and a policeman shouted, 'you had better come in here.' We did not hesitate but scrambled in quickly, it was a tight squeeze and I still don't know how we all got inside. Soon the foul air became almost unbearable, so we all decided to smoke; the struggle to get to our cigarettes couldn't have been more difficult had we been in straight-jackets. The smoke only made the atmosphere even more nauseating. One bomb crashed near enough to shake the bell-shelter. Soon after we all began drinking tea out of the policeman's thermos bottle.

Once the noise had died down and the raid had ended, we emerged and by the time we reached the aerodrome, a fierce fire was seen raging in one quarter. All of us pitched in to help put the blaze out before it could spread and before darkness fell, as we didn't want to be a target for German night bombers. Whilst some of us manned the hoses and carried buckets of water, others looked after those that had received burns or did other necessary things. Over the two days of raids, buildings had been destroyed, telephone lines blown up and the aerodrome itself cratered. But for not one instant, did it cease to be operational. For this heroic work, three of my WAAF's were later awarded Military Medals.

For her own work and courage during the enemy raids, Hanbury was later awarded the MBE. The WAAFs who were awarded decorations for their bravery under fire at Biggin Hill during the raids were Sergeant Helen Turner and Corporal Elspeth Henderson who had remained at their telephone switchboards and had continued to keep the information lines working, although their building had been hit and they had been covered in debris. The third WAAF was Sergeant Joan Mortimer who in an earlier raid had been manning the switchboard in the armoury; she had emerged with a bundle of red marker flags to help the bomb disposal teams mark out the bombs that had failed to detonate around the aerodrome, with the distinct possibility that they could go off at any time. Glen Duhig who was an orderly in the officers' mess gave his account of the raid:

> I was in charge of the Tannoy and telephone, which was located under the staircase in the hall. On the day we were bombed I was going from the mess to the airmen's mess for my meal. I was walking alongside the medical officer, when he said 'Look at those Blenheims.' They turned out to be Heinkels. We ran like mad to the sick quarters, where a blast wall had been erected and as we went in a large bomb exploded in the road alongside and this propelled us well into the building.
>
> Sometime after the attack, a German airman had been captured and was brought into the mess. He was fed a good spread, but was extremely arrogant. He spat when introduced to the pilot that had shot him down. He was detained in the guard room and Flying Officer John Stone requested that breakfast be given the next morning. I was detailed to do this and the following morning went to the guard room with a pot of coffee and all the trimmings. I met the medical orderly who gave me a bottle of cascara, which is very good for constipation. I put it in the coffee for the German, which I gather he drank, I never found out the conclusion.

With the aerodrome left in utter chaos as regards to essential services and many of the buildings no more than rubble; the job of trying to bring order back quickly to the camp was a hard task. The local army units began to set up field kitchens in the area of the South Camp to provide hot meals for the RAF ground personnel, who had begun clearing the debris and filling in the bomb craters.

Not so fortunate that day was Sergeant Henry Albert Bolton of 79 Squadron, who whilst in combat over Kenley, his aircraft V7200 was badly damaged by enemy fire and he was killed in attempting to force-land at Haliloo Farm, Woldingham, Surrey. Bolton the son of Mr and Mrs H.B. Bolton of Sunnymead, Eldon Grove, West Hartlepool; was educated at the local Technical College and the Pocklington Boys Boarding School near York, before commencing into a career in business with his grandfather and uncle of Messrs W. Bainbridge and Son. He was a keen rifleman and belonged to the local gun club. He joined the RAF Volunteer Reserve in July 1939 and completed his flying training at No.2 Flying Training School on 11th July 1940, before joining 79 Squadron at the beginning of August.

Years later, Mr C.M. Fuller who was working Haliloo Farm recalls Bolton's attempt to land his stricken Hurricane:

> The Hurricane in question crashed adjacent to the farmhouse about lunchtime. There was an air battle going on overhead and the pilot was apparently in some difficulties, had lost height and so flew up the Halliloo Valley towards Biggin Hill. He could not climb out, turned west back down the valley and stalled trying to avoid the trees.
>
> We reached him within a minute, but he was dead and seemed to have a bullet in his back and his feet had been trapped. The aircraft fell flat, but the engine was flung out on to ground a few yards away. Small parts were scattered around including the machine gun bullet belts. The local Canadians were sent to guard the machine until it was removed a few days later, extensively damaged.

Bolton was just 21 years old. His body was sent home to Hartlepool, where on Thursday 12th September a funeral service was conducted at St. Aiden's Church, West Hartlepool by the Reverend H.E. Ashdown, before he was laid to rest at Stranton Cemetery.

The other casualty that day was Australian Pilot Officer Bill Millington, who was first listed as 'Missing in action' but was later reported to be in a hospital following his shooting down by a 109. He had been chasing after a Dornier, when he was attacked by two enemy fighters; he managed to get into a position on one of the 109s and sent it crashing down over Romney Marsh; but no sooner had he watched the German pilot crawl from his smashed aircraft, when suddenly his Hurricane shuddered under the force of cannon-shells smashing into his engine. Instantaneously, flames began to blow back into his cockpit, and he quickly realised he must get out or be burnt to a cinder in a matter of moments.

As he prepared to jump by parachute, a quick glance informed him he was over a number of small villages below. He therefore decided that he would remain with the aircraft to avoid it falling and possibly killing people on the ground. He found an open field and landed his burning Hurricane. Although he was wounded in the left thigh and burnt, he managed to free himself from his aircraft, which exploded a few seconds later.

He had crash-landed on Conghurst Farm, Hawkhurst and was taken to Croydon General Hospital where he was tended for his wounds. For his bravery, he was awarded the Distinguished Flying Cross on 1st October 1940. Following his recovery, Millington was posted to No. 249 Squadron based at North Weald. Sadly he failed to return following combat with enemy aircraft on 30th October 1940, and was listed as 'Missing in action.' He was aged 23.

No. 72 Squadron lost Flying Officer Edgar Wilcox aged 23, when he was killed in combat with 109 fighters over Dungeness. Wilcox was born in nearby Croydon, and was commissioned into the Royal Air Force in November 1937. Following his flight training, he joined 72 Squadron at Church Fenton in July 1938. His Spitfire P 9457 crashed in Hungerford Field, Chickenden Farm, Staplehurst, where he was buried in All Saint's Churchyard.

The remains of one of the aerodrome's buildings following the Luftwaffe raids over 30th/31st August 1940. (Authors Collection)

A scene of devastation was witnessed, when many buildings and vehicles were destroyed or severely damaged during the two days of raid at the end of August. (Authors Collection)

Hurricane aircraft return to Biggin Hill after combat against the Luftwaffe. The ground crewman in the foreground carries a signalling flag. (Copyright IWM HU 54519A)

RAF ground personnel at Biggin Hill find time to get a bite to eat following the air-raids. Here they are pictured by the Salvation Army mobile canteen queuing for a cup of tea and a sandwich. (Bob Ogley Collection)

The three WAAFs who were each awarded the Military Medal for their outstanding bravery and devotion to duty during the Luftwaffe raids against the aerodrome are pictured with Station Commander Group Captain Richard Grice. Left to right: Sergeant Elizabeth Mortimer, Corporal Elspeth Henderson and Sergeant Helen Turner. (Copyright Imperial War Museum)

WAAF Section Officer Felicity Hanbury pictured after receiving her Military MBE at Buckingham Palace; the first woman of the war to receive this award.
(The late Dame Felicity Peake Collection)

Officers of No. 610 Squadron inspect the remains of a Messerschmitt 109 aircraft which crashed at Layhams Farm close to the aerodrome, after colliding with another Messerschmitt. Left to right: Flying Officer Brian Rees, Pilot Officer Peter Lamb and Squadron Leader John Ellis.
(Copyright No. 610 'County of Chester' Squadron Association)

Flying Officer Edgar Wilcox who served with No. 72 Squadron until he was killed in action on 31st August 1940. He is pictured here with his brother Ronald, who served with the army and was evacuated from Dunkirk. (Colin Brown Collection)

The Pilots Wings recovered from Pilot Officer Wilcox's tunic following his death. These were kept by his brother until the 1980s, when they were passed to aviation historian Colin Brown. (Colin Brown Collection)

Standing next to a Hawker Hurricane aircraft, two pilots of No. 79 Squadron. Left to right: Flying Officers George Nelson-Edwards and Douglas Clift.
(Colin Brown collection)

Sergeant Henry Albert Bolton of 79 Squadron. He was killed on 31st August,whilst attempting to crash-land his aircraft.
(Colin Brown Collection)

Pilot Officer William Millington, he was posted to No. 79 Squadron in June 1940, serving with them until he was shot down on 31st August. He failed to return from combat over the Channel on 30th October 1940. (Authors Collection)

Two pilots No. of 79 Squadron pictured at Sevenoaks Hospital after treatment, following their escape by parachute. Both were shot down on 1st September 1940. With a lovely nurse standing between them are: left Pilot Officer Brian Noble who suffered burns and Flying Officer Leofric Bryant-Fenn who was wounded in the leg. (Andy Saunders Collection)

The control column with spade-grip recovered from the crash-site excavation of Flying Officer Bryant–Fenn's Hurricane aircraft W6670.
(Colin Lee Collection)

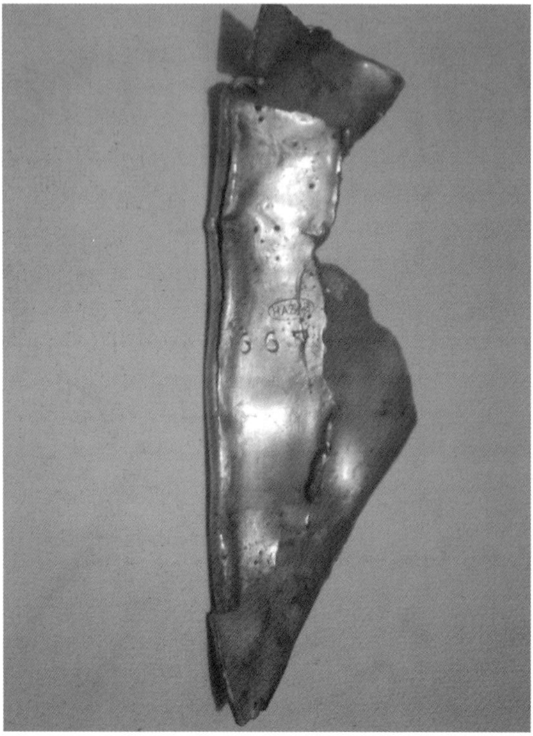

Piece of Hurricane airframe found with the aircraft's serial number W6670 that finally confirmed its identity in January 1986, following an excavation of the site in 1985.
(Colin Brown Collection)

Australian F/Lt Desmond Sheen from Sydney. He served with No. 72 Squadron, at Biggin Hill during September 1940; and was shot down twice within the space of two days during the heavy fighting. He was able to claim several enemy aircraft during this period. After the war, he remained in the RAF until his retirement in 1971 as a group captain. (Authors Collection)

Luftwaffe pilots of I/JG53 pose for a group photograph. Third from left is Oberleutnant Julius Hasse, who was shot down and killed after his parachute failed on 15th September, his Messerschmitt 109 crashed into Mullard Wood, Norshead Farm, Biggin Hill at midday. (Chris Goss Collection)

Flight Lieutenant Brian Kingcome DFC and Pilot Officer Geoffrey Wellum pictured by a 92 Squadron Spitfire. (Copyright IWM HU 112488)

Sergeant Donald 'Kingpin' Kingaby sitting on the cockpit rail of his Spitfire. He served previously with No. 266 Squadron before moving to 92 Squadron on 25th September 1940. He was to become an ace and ended the war with a total of 21 and 2 shared destroyed.
(Authors Collection)

Pilot Officer Ernest Males of No. 72 Squadron; He was shot down and killed on 27th September over Sevenoaks. (Colin Brown Collection)

Pilot Officer Norman Sutton of No.72 Squadron was killed in a collision with Sgt Staples on 5th October shortly after take-off.
( Colin Brown Collection).

Ground crewmen work on a Spitfire of 92 Squadron, September 1940.
(Copyright IWM HU 104500)

South African Adolph 'Sailor' Malan. He led No. 74 'Tiger' Squadron, when they moved into Biggin Hill in October 1940. (Authors Collection)

On 2nd October 1940, Oberleutnant Siegfried Stronk was killed when his aicraft crashed at Sutherland Avenue at Biggin Hill.
(David Brocklehurst, the Kent Battle of Britain Museum via Stronk family)

Pictured with his Messerschmitt Bf109 aircraft is Feldwebel Heinrich Hohnisch of I/JG53. Hohnisch was in combat on 9th September and was shot down. He jumped from his burning aircraft, floated down by parachute and was captured. The aircraft crashed near the Old Jail Inn, Jail Lane, Biggin Hill. (Chris Goss Collection)

Tony Bartley flew with No. 92 Squadron throughout 1940; he became an ace pilot during this period with 8 victories, He later became a flight commander and a production test pilot for Vickers-Supermarine This is the pencil portrait of him drawn by the artist Cuthbert Orde. After the war, he was married to the film actress Deborah Kerr, they divorced in 1958; he followed a career in film and television production.

(Authors Collection)

Pilots of No. 92 Squadron who served at Biggin Hill from September 1940 into 1941. Left to right: Flying Officer Garland (Engineering Officer), Flying Officer Tom Weiss (Intelligence Officer), Pilot Officer Roy Mottram, Sergeant Ralph Havercroft. Flight Liutenant Brian Kingcome, Squadron Leader Johnny Kent, Flying Officer Tom Sherrington, Pilot Officer Cecil Saunders, Flying Officer Robert Holland, Flying Officer Allan Wright, Sergeant Hugh Bowen-Morris and Sergeant John Lund.
(Author via the late Tony Bartley)

Two of No. 74 Tiger' Squadron's ace pilots; Flight Lieutenant John Mungo-Park DFC and Flying Officer Harbourne Mackay Stephen DFC, who shared in the destruction of the 600th enemy aircraft destroyed of the war by a Biggin Hill squadron. (Authors Collection)

Pictured celebrating Biggin Hill's 600th enemy aircraft destroyed on 30th November 1940; Flying Officer Stephen and Flight Lieutenant Mungo Park chat with other pilots of the squadron. Behind them is Pilot Officer Edward Churches and far right is Henryk Szczesny known as 'Henry the Pole.' (Pathe News)

Sergeant Jack Hammerton of 615 Squadron was killed on 6th November 1940, whilst undertaking a patrol in his Hurricane over Biggin Hill.
(The National Archive, London)

Sergeant Peter Willcocks of No. 66 Squadron. He was tragically killed in a collision with Flying Officer Hubert 'Dizzy' Allen on 28th November 1940.
(Colin Brown Collection)

Flight Lieutenant Robert 'Bobby' Oxspring a flight commander with No. 66 Squadron pictured at Biggin in November 1940.
(Author via The late Robert Oxspring)

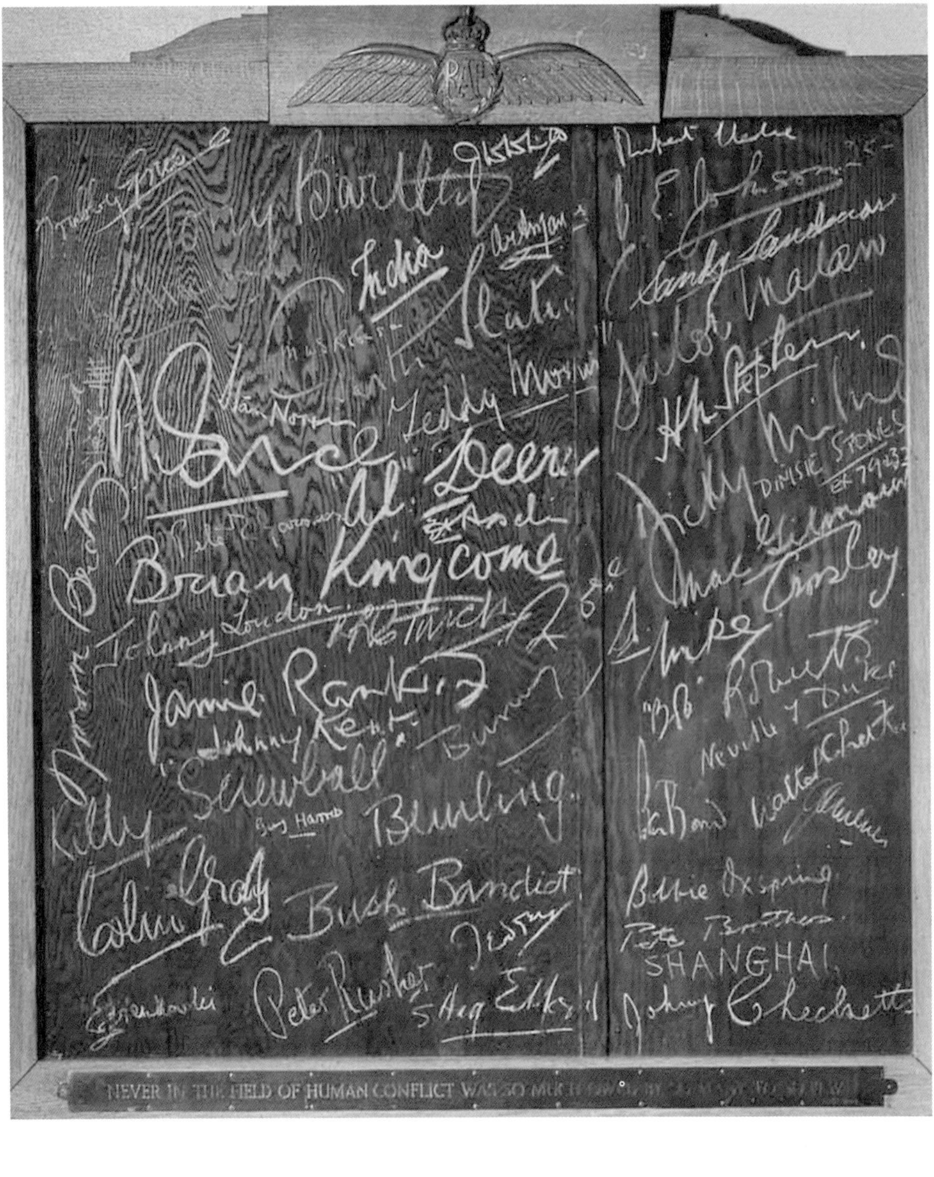


The famous White Hart Pub black-out board that was signed by many of the fighter pilots who served at Biggin Hill during the Battle of Britain and later in the war. (Copyright RAF Museum, Hendon, London)

# Chapter 6
# September
# 1940

At 2.00 pm on 1st September, eleven Hurricanes of 79 Squadron were ordered to scramble and patrol Biggin Hill, when a large formation of enemy aircraft was picked up and heading towards the vicinity of the aerodrome. They intercepted the formation and individual combats with the bombers and their Messerschmitt escort ensued. Following the battle, the South African pilot Flight Lieutenant Geoffrey Haysom damaged a Dornier, but was himself hit by enemy fire which damaged his aircraft, he crashed on landing back at the aerodrome, but was uninjured. Pilot Officer 'Dimsie' Stones claimed two Dorniers as probably destroyed, Pilot Officer Mayhew confirmed his Dornier 17 as destroyed and Pilot Officer Douglas Clift reported a Messerschmitt that he had shot at as a probable. One of the pilots flying this patrol was Pilot Officer Paul Mayhew; his combat report relays the following:

> A large force of bombers was sighted, but I was unable to reach their height. When I had climbed to 15,000 feet, I saw about 12 Dornier's escorted by an equal number of Messerschmitt 110s over Westerham flying north-west. The fighters appeared to be already engaged, so I attacked the bomber formation from in front and to the left. The third aircraft of the leading Vic formation turned head on to me. As we passed I turned sharply and came on its tail. I was attacked from astern by an unknown fighter, but succeeded in shaking him off. I returned to undertake a port-quarter attack on the Dornier and opened fire at 230 yards, holding an 8-second burst until I broke away at a range of 75-yards. I saw tracer entering the cockpit and engines. His port engine let out smoke as he soared

upwards, stalled and went into a quick spin. I followed the aircraft down and saw it crash in the corner of a wood, two miles south-east of Westerham. It exploded violently and burnt out.

The German aircraft destroyed by Mayhew belonged to 15/LG1 with the loss of both crew, crashing at Hosey Wood, Chartwell.

Pilot Officer Brian Noble also of No. 79 Squadron was also in combat, and recounts being shot down during this sortie:

I remember being recalled from the Officers' Mess after a vain attempt to eat a hurried lunch, and being 'scrambled' immediately on arriving back at dispersal. Subsequently, during the climb we intercepted a large Luftwaffe bomber formation and made a somewhat hurried attack, although to what effect I cannot remember as I found myself crossing through the formation at a height of 12, 000 to 15,000 feet, surrounded by enemy aircraft, tracer and cannon fire.

Whilst turning left to run through the enemy formation, I felt a dull thud and simultaneously saw a burst of flame below my feet, indicating a hit in the main fuel tank behind the instrument panel. My remaining memory is of releasing the locking pin on my harness, pushing the stick hard forward to convert the turn into a 'bunt,' the effect of which was to project me out of the cockpit, having already previously opened the canopy hood. I recall having some trouble pulling the parachute ripcord, my hands having been burned and losing some nails on both hands. I recall only two brief moments whilst parachuting down, one of being close to another parachuting airman and both of us being investigated by a friendly fighter, the other of being over water into which I fell almost immediately.

This in fact was the Marley sand/gravel pit at Riverhead, Sevenoaks and from which I was promptly rescued by the local LDV, one of whom took me to the local hospital at Sevenoaks, where I was to spend the next month with Flying Officer Trevor

Bryant-Fenn, my section leader on that sortie. After one month in Sevenoaks, I was moved to Torquay and later to the burns unit at the Queen Victoria Hospital at East Grinstead. I never did find out what happened to my Hurricane *P2062.

*Brian Noble's aircraft was actually (L2062). Pilot Officer Trevor Bryant-Fenn also recalls that day's encounter with the enemy:

Biggin Hill was under regular air attack at this time, so pilots were dispersed at night. I and two others spent the previous night at the home of Sir Waldron Smithers MP at Knockholt. I well recall chatting with Sir Waldron and Lady Smithers in their garden after breakfast before returning to the airfield. It was a beautiful sunny morning, not a cloud in the sky.

There had already been a lot of air activity on Sunday 1st September and the readiness aircraft were airborne. At about mid-day an order came through to scramble all available aircraft to patrol over Biggin at 20,000 feet. There were only two aircraft, mine W6670 and the other flown by Brian Noble. We took off and gained height and at about 17,000 feet saw a mass of aircraft with fighter cover above us and heading for London.

We climbed to their height and identified about thirty Dornier 17s with Me109s behind and above. Brian Noble was echelon starboard to me. I got a Dornier in my sights and pressed the firing button, when tracer fire started overtaking me from behind. I felt a thump on my leg and a fire started down by my right rudder pedal. Flames started to build up in my cockpit, so I decided to quit. The next thing I remember is being on the end of my parachute and some Me109s milling around with another parachute not far away. I landed at Dunton Green and later met up with Brian Noble in the same ward at Sevenoaks hospital.

Bryant-Fenns Hurricane W6670 fell to earth, crashing at Grays Road on the top of Westerham Hill, south of the aerodrome. The aircraft become the subject of an excavation in 1985, but no positive identification aircraft numbers were found. It was eventually identified a few weeks later the site was re-visited by Battle of Britain historian Colin Brown of the Croydon Aviation Research Group, when a piece of airframe with the aircraft's serial number was found.

For the next couple of days it was fairly quiet, with 79 Squadron undertaking a number of patrols during both the mornings and afternoons, but there was nothing to report in regards to enemy air activity. The squadron was scrambled during the afternoon of the 4th September at 1.10 pm, when enemy activity was plotted coming in over the Kent coast. Six Hurricanes climbed into the sky and were vectored on to the enemy formation, they claimed a number of bombers damaged and one Messerschmitt 110 destroyed, shot down by Flying Officer George Peters.

Following their return to Biggin, one aircraft was reported missing; this was Sergeant John Wright's aircraft, Hurricane P3676, which had been severely damaged by return fire from the enemy bombers. Wright had also been wounded and tried desperately to make a forced landing in a sports field at the village of Tolworth, near Kingston-upon-Thames, but he abandoned this idea because he had seen a group of children playing below. He eventually in desperation put down his aircraft at the end of a cul-de-sac at Wentworth Close, Long Ditton. He was pulled from his aircraft and rushed to a local hospital, where sadly he died of his injuries the next day. Aged 24 years, his body was sent home to his family and he was buried in the New Kilpatrick Cemetery, Dunbartonshire.

Robert Deacon Elliott of 72 Squadron, temporally had to fly from Croydon and recalls:

> Because the aerodrome at Biggin was so badly damaged from the previous day's raids, the squadron was sent to Croydon to operate, until Biggin was functional again. While at Croydon, Flying Officer Desmond Sheen was shot down, but landed safely by parachute, Flight Lieutenant Ron Thomson and Flying Officer Oswald Pigg were both listed as missing; Sergeant Maurice Pocock was badly

> shot up. I was myself hit by a Me109, but I managed to get back, the aircraft was badly damaged with lots of holes in the wings and so on. 'Happy' Thomson was later reported to be in hospital. Sadly Oswald Pigg was finally reported as killed.

Desmond Sheen also remembers this period:

> We were moved to Croydon only a few miles away. I was on my third sortie from Croydon to intercept a bunch of Heinkels and I was attacking one when I was shot down by a 109 I never saw. I had to bale out and landed in a field near Maidstone.

Flight Lieutenant Ted Graham who was leading one of the squadrons flights during this time, remembers Oswald Pigg and Edgar Wilcox who had been killed on the 31st August.

> Both Pigg and Wilcox possessed formidable personalities, both were lively companions. Oswald revealed a quick dry wit and Edgar a more direct conversational style, who pulled no punches should he feel strongly enough. Both never failed to meet their duty calls, and were always amongst the first ready to scramble. Both would never fail to press home their attacks on their 'Jerry' targets to finality, and were therefore more open to being jumped by other circling 109s, this is what I think happened to them.
>
> I was lucky myself on 2nd September, when my Spitfire X4241 was hit in the fuel tank with incendiaries, or explosive bullets and was forced to land at Lympne on the heights above Romney, where the runway was bomb cratered. Blinded by smoke and fumes I ran into a crater. When finding my way to HQ I heard a sort of coughing sound from above and looking up I saw a Hurricane descending without a propeller. It made a perfect landing avoiding all the craters. The prop had been lost by being hit by a cannon-firing 109 at right angles. I made my way back to base by train carrying my chute.

Biggin received two more raids on 3rd September, one during the early morning at 7.30 am and another at 10.30 am. This caused further damage to the roads within the aerodrome perimeter, once again all communications and services were cut. Not one building now stood undamaged.

The next day, the Station Commander Richard Grice viewed his aerodrome from aloft, when he was flown in a Miles Magister aircraft to inspect the damage that the enemy had inflicted over the last four days. Looking down, he observed the devastation that the Luftwaffe had inflicted; there was only one of the three hangars still intact which looked undamaged from the air. On landing, he decided to take drastic action to stop the Luftwaffe targeting his aerodrome. If the enemy could see that there was nothing left to destroy and the aerodrome looked out of action, this would hopefully dissuade any further raids.

He got together his Engineer Officer Flight Lieutenant Jackson and soldiers of the Royal Engineers and told him of his plan to destroy the last remaining hangar. After evacuating that area of the aerodrome and planting demolition charges, everybody was ordered to take cover. At 6.00 pm, the demolition charge plunger was pushed and a massive explosion deafened those in the vicinity, followed by a large cloud of smoke and flying debris that billowed into the air. Once the cloud and dust had settled, the ground personnel were able to view what was left of the hangar.

Unfortunately for Group Captain Grice, his actions that day would have unforeseen consequences. Later, the Air Ministry who were far from impressed with his actions, ordered that he face a court of enquiry for his unorthodox action in destroying property belonging to the Royal Air Force.

At 10.00 am on the morning of the 5th September, the sirens sounded over the aerodrome to alert all personnel to prepare for another enemy attack. Six aircraft of 'B' Flight 79 Squadron took to the air immediately. The enemy force was intercepted before reaching its target and was driven off. Flight Lieutenant Geoffrey Haysom landed back at Biggin with his wings port aileron badly damaged by enemy bullets. The pilots reported that they had met a formation consisting of forty bombers with an escort of fifty to sixty fighters at a height of 15,000 feet. 79 suffered no casualties that day. 72 Squadron were also called upon during that day as Desmond Sheen recalled:

> We were sent to operate from our forward base at Hawkinge. We landed at and refuelled, during which time the airfield was attacked and we spent some time in the air-raid shelters. We then eventually took off; I was leading at the time when I received a warning over the radio of 'Bandits above' but it was to late and I was badly hit. I passed out and when I came to, I was falling vertically with half a wing gone and no control whatsoever, so I pulled the release on my seat harness and as I immediately broke free, I pulled the ripcord. I landed and was taken to the Queen Mary's Hospital in Sidcup, where I was hospitalised for a couple of weeks.

72 Squadron suffered the loss of two pilots killed during that day, Pilot Officer Douglas Winter and Sergeant Malcolm Gray. Winter was flying Spitfire X4013, when he was attacked by enemy fighters, his aircraft was at a too low altitude for him to use a parachute and he was killed. The aircraft crashed at Covert Wood, Elham. Sergeant Gray crashed into Elham Wood in Spitfire N3093.

Pilot Officer Robert Deacon Elliott kept a diary and wrote down the following for 6th September:

> 6th Sept 40: Only five Spitfires available first thing today; the lowest number the squadron has operated since the war began. We were up on an early patrol, saw a lot of enemy aircraft, but did not engage; they were out of reach and well on their way home acting as a rear-guard protection to some straggling bombers.
>
> Only four aircraft available for the next mission, so we joined up with No.66 Squadron and the Kenley Wing. It was over Ashford, south-east Kent that we ran into some bombers, escorted as usual by many Me109s. We were terribly outnumbered. In making two

consecutive head-on attacks on a Me109, he went down smoking and crashed near Marden, killing the pilot.

In the process my aircraft was too badly damaged, the bullet proof windscreen splintered and the leading edges of the wings were holed and torn, and very shortly afterwards, when down to 1,000 feet something exploded, blowing off my engine cowling. My Spitfire caught fire, I baled-out from 800 feet and landing in a hop field only to find I was being covered by a shot gun in the hands of a member of a Local Defence Volunteer.

The hop pickers I remember gave me their remaining last bottle of beer – how refreshing. They seemed perturbed at the number of RAF planes being shot down around their area, they had hoped for more Germans. The army very kindly collected me and had me driven back to base.

Sunday 7th September, was a day which would completely change the tide of the battle. Only several nights earlier, Winston Churchill had given Bomber Command explicit instructions to hit back at the heart of Germany, Berlin. Eighty-one Hampden twin-engine light bombers dropped their bombs on the German capital and other industrial targets including the Siemens factory.

This raid was in reprisal for an attack made by the Luftwaffe on the previous night of 25th August, when during a mission to bomb installations around Chatham, Rochester and Thames Haven oil refineries. The bombers of Luftflotte 2 had mistakenly dropped their bomb loads over central London. Areas hit during that night included Islington and Finsbury in North London, Stepney, Bethnal Green and East Ham in the East End.

The British reprisal had so outraged Hitler that he immediately ordered his Reichmarschall Herman Goring to make immediate plans for the bombing of London, both by day and by night; thus bringing Britain to its knees and surrender terms.

Herman Goring decided he would personally take full command of the planning for the attacks on London, overruling his main commanders

Generalfieldmarschalls Albert Kesselring and Hugo Sperrle. Goring travelled to Calais in his own personal train to set up his headquarters and witness at first hand the aerial assault against London.

The weather that day dawned fine over the south-east although there was some mist over the Channel, but this soon cleared to give perfect flying weather. The morning saw little air activity apart from a few German reconnaissance aircraft sorties.

At the RAF plotting rooms there was no sign of any enemy formations building up across the Channel over in France and squadrons were kept at readiness most of the day, waiting for the call to scramble. At around 4.00 pm, the alarm bells sounded when radar stations began picking up formations forming over the Calais area of over twenty-plus aircraft. The RAF commanders assumed that the raids would again head for targets such as airfields and installations and all fighters were scrambled to patrol these areas.

Goring in the meantime had gathered his staff to a forward position overlooking the Channel at Calais and viewed through his binoculars his vast armada of bombers and fighter escorts, as they roared overhead towards the white cliffs of Kent, onwards towards their target, London. Vast formations stepped up at various altitudes consisting of over three hundred bombers with an escort of six hundred fighters headed out in two waves. The first wave would head for the Thames Estuary and the second would follow heading directly for London.

This caused confusion within RAF Fighter Command as to the Luftwaffe's real target and heading. All to soon and to late, it was recognised that London was the target and fighter squadrons had to be re-deployed urgently to cover the capital.

Those squadrons covering sector aerodromes were hurriedly despatched to try and intercept the bombers who were now closing in over London and preparing to drop their bombs. Some RAF fighters managed to intercept and engage, but they were heavily pressed by the Messerschmitt 109s and 110s that provided close escort from above and alongside their bomber comrades. On the run into London, the German aircraft ran the gauntlet of the anti-aircraft defences within and around the capital, sending up black puffs of flak across the late summer sky.

Once over the target area, the bombs rained down; first on the London dock area of Millwall, Silvertown and Limehouse and then further up towards London Bridge. Vast warehouses full of timber, sugar and other inflammable produce were set ablaze, causing the flames and smoke to be seen for miles and giving the incoming German air fleet a perfect beacon to guide them in.

At 4.40 pm one raid was observed coming in the direction of Biggin Hill aerodrome. Six aircraft of 'B' Flight 79 Squadron were sent off to cover the aerodrome as the formation of Junkers Ju88s, Dornier 17s and 215s drew near. Pilot Officer Donald Stones with Squadron Leader John Heyworth claimed a Junkers bomber as probably destroyed as did Pilot Officer Peters. Pilot Officer Stones failed to return from the sortie and was listed as missing, but it was later learnt that day that he had received a bullet wound in one leg, and had landed safely at West Malling airfield. 72 Squadron was also in the thick of the action and encountered a formation of 100-plus enemy aircraft, east of Rochester flying at 22,000 feet at 5.00 pm. The formation consisted of Heinkels and Messerschmitt 109s. Flying Officer John Wolferstan Villa was flying in 'Red Section' and claimed one of the bombers, as his combat report relates:

> I was flying as Red 1 and had my section astern of 'Tennis' leader with two aircraft weaving over the top. On sighting the enemy, our leader ordered us into individual line astern, and then echelon starboard on approaching the enemy aircraft. We approached the enemy bomber force from the side. I attacked a Heinkel from below and the quarter. I opened fire at 150- yards and continued firing until my aircraft stalled and fell away. The bomber broke away from the formation and started to dive. I experienced very heavy fire from the enemy aircraft, both machine gun and canon. My aircraft was undamaged. I did not recover control of my aircraft until I was down to 5,000 feet. I then saw Red 2, Sergeant

> White make a force-landing and circled around him in case enemy fighters should attack him. I then started to climb up again, but received orders that all aircraft should land, refuel and re-arm as quickly as possible. I returned and landed at base.

From this sortie, 72 Squadron claimed one German aircraft destroyed and one probable plus a damaged. Flight Lieutenant Thomas Elsdon who had been leading the squadron was hit by enemy fire in Spitfire X4254, he was wounded badly in the left knee and right shoulder. He decided that rather than bale-out, he would head for Biggin Hill. He could not lower his undercarriage due to damage and carried out a crash-landing.

He was quickly rushed to hospital and remained there until he recovered, but was not operationally fit until July 1941; when he joined No. 257 Squadron based at Coltishall in Norfolk. Sergeant John White, whose forced-landing had been witnessed by John Villa, brought his aircraft R7022 to land at Eynsford, suffering slight injuries to his forehead and one leg. While serving with No.73 Squadron serving in the Western Desert on 14th June 1941, while trying to get his damaged Hurricane fighter back to base; it stalled and spun in, crashing at Sidi Barrani. He died aged 25 from injuries and was buried at Halfaya Sollum War cemetery, Egypt.

As darkness drew in that evening, all one could see for miles around was the glow of the flames that lit up the night sky over London. Even as far as the Thames Estuary coast, people could make out the brightness in the night sky emanating from the capital.

The raids continued through the night until 5.00am the next morning, causing death and destruction never witnessed before on mainland Britain. The bombing had killed 430 civilians and seriously injured 1,600 others. The Luftwaffe had dropped 330 tons of high explosive and 440 tons of fire starting incendiaries. The blitz on London had begun.

The following morning, Londoners emerged from their shelters to witness the devastation of burnt out and demolished buildings that were once their homes and work place. But undaunted, life had to go on and the process of carrying on with normal life as best they could began.

On the 8th September, 79 Squadron received orders to pull out of Biggin Hill and fly to Pembrey in South Wales for a well-earned rest. They would not return to Biggin Hill again having been operational from the drome since March 1937.

A new squadron arrived at Biggin Hill to take the place of 79 Squadron, when No. 92 'East India' Squadron who flew in from Pembrey led by their commanding officer, Squadron Leader Phillip Sanders. There they had seen little action at Pembrey, only the occasional German bomber which came over mainly at night. Their radio call-sign was 'Gannic'

Within the squadron there were a number of excellent fighter pilots who had previously seen action over Dunkirk in May 1940 and had claimed a number of victories; these included Flight Lieutenant Brian Kingcome, a squared faced individual who pre-war had joined the RAF as a cadet and attended RAF Cranwell Collage. While at Cranwell, he had been involved in a car accident, his face and nose had been smashed; but after several weeks recuperating he resumed his course before being sent to his first posting with No. 65 Squadron in 1937 at Hornchurch.

There was also Tony Bartley, of Irish descent, a very good looking individual and a very good pilot as was Allan Wright who was a thin, blonde haired slight individual, who seemed to be the quite type, but once in the cockpit was again an aggressive fighter pilot. Tony Bartley later recalled the squadron's first days at the aerodrome:

> We arrived at Biggin, where we were thrown immediately into the battle straight away, doing up to five sorties a day; we never stopped. You went to your dispersal hut, just before dawn and scrambled when the Tannoy sounded and fought all day long until the sun went down. At the end of the day, we use to get off the airfield because Jerry would sometimes come over and bomb us at night. We use to go down to the White Hart Pub at Brasted and drink beer.

Brian Kingcome would also later recall the early days at the aerodrome:

We arrived at Biggin Hill led by our CO Phillip Sanders, Bob Tuck had been posted away to lead a Hurricane squadron up at Coltishall. In those days people were promoted in fighter squadrons on seniority, which was the normal peace-time thing; which was not working because basically you really needed somebody who had operational experience and had a fair amount of flying under their belt. 'Sandy' Sanders was a very nice chap and had come in to take over and was a well correct and behaved officer, but he lacked the experience.

I remember he came down to dispersal soon after landing from a sortie. His aircraft had been damaged during the encounter and his clothing had been soaked in 100–octane fuel. He lit his only cigarette of the day and immediately burst into flames; so he was carried off and went to hospital suffering from burns and I became acting commander.

I led the squadron for two or three weeks, then we got another chap named Lister, who had a decoration for being on the North-West Frontier, so he got his experience of operational flying by chasing the tribesmen and dropping bombs on the villages. He acted as my wingman for about two sorties before he was shot down and ended up in hospital.

The very next day following their arrival at Biggin, 92 was action. During late afternoon of 9th September, they took off to patrol and at 5.00pm encountered a large formation of enemy bombers and fighters 15,000 feet north of Biggin Hill; they were heading in towards London. Brian Kingcome recorded the sortie that day:

I got separated from the squadron while proceeding to our objective, but by following the vectors I had heard, I saw a large formation of enemy bombers. They were already being attacked by a squadron of Spitfires as I climbed up. There were 12 yellow-nosed 109s which were circling in line astern above and to the

> left of the bombers. I joined in and gave the last machine a short burst from my guns. He dived away from the formation with smoke coming back. He then turned on his back and dived away. I dived into cloud and returned to base as my oxygen supply was exhausted. I claimed the 109 as a probable.

The squadron had two aircraft written off that day due to enemy action; Spitfire L1077 flown by Pilot Officer Cecil Saunders had his rudder shot away and crash-landed at Whitehouse Farm, Romney Marsh. He suffered wounds to a leg and was treated by the Royal Army Medical Corps at Brooklands on Romney Marsh; more seriously injured was Pilot Officer William Watling who was forced to jump from his burning Spitfire P9372 after combat with 109s. He was burned on the face and hands and landed by parachute into the sea off Winchelsea beach. He was rescued and admitted to hospital, where he remained for two months before returning to the squadron. He was to lose his life on 7th February 1941 when his Spitfire flew into a hill due to bad visibility at Kingsdown, near Deal. He is buried at St. Mary's Cray Cemetery, Orpington.

One enemy aircraft that was shot down that day crashed nearby to the aerodrome. This was a Messerschmitt 109 Werke No. 1508 of 1/JG53. This was shot down by RAF fighters at approximately 6.00 pm and was being flown by Feldwebel Heinrich Hohnisch; he managed to bale out south of the airfield landing north of Westerham, before his aircraft crashed into the ground at Cherry Tree Farm near the Old Jail Inn, Jail Lane, Biggin Hill.

92 Squadron was airborne on 11th September at 4.00 pm and intercepted a large enemy formation at an altitude of between 20,000 to 25,000 feet consisting of Heinkel He111s with a mixed escort of 109s and 110s. The squadron went into attack as the formation was over Dungeness. Pilot Officer Williams wrote of the interception in his combat report:

> I was flying as 'Green 2' on patrol over Maidstone. After the

> squadron had broken up individually at 'Angels 15' I saw a Heinkel being attacked by another Spitfire (Pilot Officer Wade) at about 12,000 feet. I joined in the attack with the other Spitfire. We succeeded in first making his starboard engine useless and forcing him down until it crashed through a hedge in a field and came to a standstill. I did a beam, a quarter and a head on attack on the Heinkel. I observed fire at first from the rear-gunner, but it later stopped. After crashing, three of the crew got out and dragged the forth to a hedge. Civilians then appeared on the scene. The aircraft was painted black and had a large white striped square on the starboard wing and the letter 'A' in white along the fuselage. The position of crash was somewhere near Lympne.

Also flying on that sortie was young 19 year old Pilot Officer Geoffrey Wellum; he had joined the Royal Air Force the year before, in August 1939; joining No. 92 Squadron in May 1940, when based at RAF Northolt. He had survived the fighter operations over Dunkirk and was probably one of the youngest pilots in the Battle of Britain. Known to his comrades as 'Boy' Wellum; he claimed a German bomber this day:

> Having lost the squadron, I was flying near to the coast at 9,000 feet, when I sighted and engaged a Heinkel 111. The port engine was out of action. I did one quarter attack and was immediately met with gunfire from the top and bottom guns from the aircraft. I carried out a second attack and was met by fire from only the top gunner. Black smoke began to pour from the starboard engine. I did one more quarter attack and then went in from astern. White smoke came forth from the starboard engine and the enemy aircraft began to lose height slowly. Having expended all of my ammunition I broke off the engagement and headed for base.

No. 92 Squadron lost two pilots that day, Pilot Officer Harry Edwards who had taken off from the aerodrome with seven other Spitfires to provide escort for bombers on raid over the Channel to attack the

French ports. He was shot down when they met a large formation of Messerschmitt 109s at 7.00 pm. After the combat, Edwards was reported as missing. It was not until 7th October that notification was received from Hawkinge that his body had been found at Evegate Manor Farm, Smeeth, near Ashford. The wreckage was seen to crash by an eye-witness in a field and that his body was still in the wreckage, he must have been killed instantaneously on impact with the ground. The crash-site was left for weeks until it was apparent that nobody was coming to recover the aircraft. Eventually, his body was recovered by the Home Guard and he was buried at Hawkinge on 10th October.

The other loss was of Pilot Officer Frederick Norman Hargreaves aged 21. He was listed as missing in action following combat with enemy fighter at 3.20 pm that afternoon. Presumably, he and his Spitfire K9793 crashed into the sea off Dungeness. His body was never found and he listed on the Runnymede Memorial Panel 8.

The only other casualty that day was Flying Officer James Paterson, he was shot down in Spitfire R6613 by 109s, but managed to bale-out with his uniform on fire and he was badly burned about the face. His aircraft crashed north-east of Ashford. After treatment, he returned to the squadron and insisted on flying operationally once more before he could properly see.

Following the mornings engagement, during which 92 Squadron had suffered the loss of two experienced pilots and a third with injuries, the squadron was called into the air again at 11.45 am and for a third time at 2.45 pm. They took off in company with No. 66 Squadron; led once more by Kingcome and over Sevenoaks sighted a formation of Junkers Ju88s at 15,000 feet.

Another fighter squadron returned once again to Biggin Hill on 13th September, but their stay would be extremely brief. The squadron was No. 141 who had suffered very high casualties in July. 'B' Flight arrived from RAF Church Fenton during the afternoon flying Boulton Paul Defiant aircraft. Two aircraft of 'B' Flight flew over to operate from the small airfield at Gatwick, under the control of Kenley's Operations Room.

During the morning of 14th September, 72 Squadron were called into action, when enemy bombers and fighters were picked up. They intercepted them as they headed back across the Channel, but none of the pilots were able to claim in knocking down any of the enemy. Later that afternoon both 72 and 92 Squadrons encountered a large formation of Messerschmitt 109s and they were more successful as the combat report filed by Sergeant William Rolls of 'Blue' Section reported his action during this flight.

> I took off from Biggin Hill at 18.00 as Blue 3 and we were told to patrol Canterbury at 20,000 feet. We met the enemy west of Canterbury as we were about to get in line astern to attack, a Me109 dived down from behind and started to do a quarter attack on Blue 2 as he was going under Blue 1. He had fired a few rounds at Blue 2, then I was in a position to do a quarter attack on the Me109. I was at 150 yards range approximately, when I opened fire. I gave a 4-second burst with full deflection and saw my bullets and tracer sweep down the side of the 109. It suddenly pulled back as though to do a loop and then spun down with what appeared to be glycol fumes coming from it. I watched it spin from 6,000 feet then suddenly another Spitfire flew up to it, so I left it to him in case it wanted finishing, while I went back to try and make contact again. The Me109 eventually crashed in flames at Betherston, after the other pilot had put another burst into it.

The Messerschmitt in question was in fact an aircraft of 6/LG2 Werke No. 2014, piloted by Unteroffizier Blazejewski, he fortunately baled-out, landed safely without injury and was captured. His aircraft eventually crashed at Thanet Wood on New Street Farm, Great Chart, near Ashford at 6.35 pm.

Pilot Officer Allan Wright of 92 Squadron was able to claim one of the 109s as damaged as did Brian Kingcome who claimed a further two as damaged. Wright's report states:

> Took off from Biggin Hill, as Green 1 at 18.00 hours, after receiving some vectors. While approximately over Tonbridge, I saw about 30 Me109s at 3,000 feet above our formation and travelling in the opposite direction. We were at 18,000 feet with the sun behind us and had been 7,000 feet higher. We should have surprised them, an earlier take off and climb over base would have made this possible. As it was, they saw us and having passed over us into the sun began their attacks by peeling off in twos. I saw four coming past me and turning on to my tail as I was climbing. I did as best a turn as I could without stalling and got in a two second burst at two of them as the third opened fire on me. I saw tracer going into one of them, but could not see the result of my fire, because as I tried to turn back on to them, I spun and when I pulled out I could find no sign of them, only part of another Spitfire Squadron. Therefore I turned southwards and patrolled the coast to catch any returning raiders, but as there were none I returned to base.

The 15th September 1940, is now official recorded as being at the height of the Battle of Britain and is commemorated in Britain as Battle of Britain Day.

On this day the pilots were up early as usual and at readiness waiting for instructions to get airborne from their various group controllers. The weather that morning was ideal with clear visibility, perfect flying weather.

Strangely, no enemy activity had been observed and by 10.00 am, Fighter Command Headquarters wondered what the Germans were planning next. However news was relayed to Sector Stations from RAF Headquarters at 11.33 am that radar had picked up German aircraft gathering over the south-east of Boulogne, turning out across the Channel heading for the English coast between Dover and Folkestone. Immediately fighter squadrons in 11 Group were scrambled to intercept the threat. The Duxford Wing was called into action soon afterwards and instructed by control to patrol over the Gravesend and Canterbury line.

One victim of that raid was Staffel Kapitan Oberleutnant Julius Hasse of 3/JG53, He was shot down during combat at midday just outside London. His Messerschmitt 109 Werke No. 1590 was badly hit and he had no alternative but to take to his parachute; unfortunately his parachute for some reason failed to open and he fell to his death at Luxsted Hall Lane. His aircraft dived into Mollards Wood, Norheads Farm at Biggin Hill. He was claimed by Sergeant George Unwin of 19 Squadron. Pilot Officer Geoffrey Gaunt flying with No. 609 Squadron was shot down by enemy fighters at 12.15 am south-east of London. His aircraft R6690, and spun down at Still's Farm, Addington.

During the afternoon of 15th September, Pilot Officer Roy Mottram of 92 Squadron was flying in the position of 'Blue 2' when the squadron was scrambled to intercept the enemy at 2.30 pm. During this engagement he was able to claim a Heinkel destroyed and a Dornier damaged; as his report describes:

> I was Blue 2 and ordered to patrol with 92 Squadron over Hornchurch at 10,000 feet. Becoming separated from the rest of the squadron I climbed into the sun until I reached 20,000 feet. I then saw a formation of Hurricanes to the east, also further east was a mass of about 70 aircraft. About 5,000 feet below were several Dornier 17s. I chased one to the top of the clouds and opened fire on its starboard engine from 200 yards. As it went into cloud, I closed up to about 40 yards and gave each engine a 5-second burst from my guns. As visibility was bad, I could not see any effect and I eventually lost it in the thick clouds. I then flew through the cloud and waited beneath at 6,000 feet. After a few minutes, a Heinkel appeared and I did a quarter attack on its starboard engine. Smoke came from it and after two more attacks flames appeared. It began to lose height rapidly and I watched it crash in a field in the Ashford district.

The fresh faced 20-year old New Zealander, Pilot Officer Howard Perry Hill from Christchurch was also in the thick of the action:

> I carried out three beam attacks on a Dornier over Hornchurch, firing short bursts until I was within 30 yards before breaking away. I left the enemy aircraft after one of the crew baled-out and the machine began smoking. I then noticed a Heinkel heading east just above the cloud level. I carried out a couple of beam attacks from slightly ahead of the enemy aircraft before I broke away once again. This aircraft crashed on the edge of a wood, south of the estuary and exploded; the crew had baled-out. I climbed once more and delivered another attack on another Heinkel, which after two of my attacks landed with its undercarriage up on a local aerodrome. I was about to enter cloud, when I saw a Heinkel bomber coming through. I carried out two beam attacks and one from the stern before it finally crashed behind a row of houses near Rochester.

Three of 92 Squadrons pilots had suffered at the hands of the Luftwaffe that day; Flight Sergeant Sydney returned with Spitfire R6767, with one of the wings badly shot up with gaping holes from 20 mm cannon shells. Pilot Officer Tony Bartley in Spitfire P9513, had been badly damaged after engaging Dornier bombers over Ashford, but managed to limp home. Pilot Officer Bob Holland had to take to his parachute after his Spitfire R6606 was shot down west of Ashford. He injured himself on landing and was taken to the East Grinstead hospital for treatment

At approximately 6.20 pm, a Bristol Beaufighter of No. 25 Squadron with the Serial No. R2067 crashed near to the aerodrome at Leaves Green, killing three of the aircrew, Pilot Officer Miles John Miley, Flying Officer Hugh Michael Lambert and Leading Aircraftsman J.P. Wyatt. Hugh Lambert's sister Felicity later recalled the accident:

> He was always known as Mike; the Royal Air Force was his life and he went straight from school and after qualifying as a fighter pilot and getting his commission, he became a member of 25 Squadron

in the 1930s at Hawkinge.

The day of the accident, he was flying Pilot Officer Miles Miley to Biggin Hill from North Weald to pick up another aircraft, which Michael was then to fly on to the Bristol Aircraft Company at Filton for repairs. Whilst this aircraft was being serviced, he was to have had 48-hours leave at home as we lived only three miles from Filton; we were waiting there with a car to pick him up for a well-earned rest. The Beaufighter had been equipped with the latest secret air radar equipment known as A.I. (airborne interception). The exact details of the crash were never disclosed. We never found out if it was a flying accident or if he had been shot down?

During the evening of the 15/16th, one aircraft from No.141 Squadron was given instructions to patrol at midnight. During this flight two enemy aircraft were encountered, one was destroyed and one claimed as probably destroyed; both falling to the guns of Air Gunner Sergeant Alfred Cumbers and his pilot Flying Officer John Waddingham. On return to Gatwick, they were heartily congratulated by their ground crews and fellow officers. John Waddingham's combat report states:

During a clear moonlight, with 20/25 miles visibility we patrolled a line between Maidstone and Tunbridge at a height of 9,000 feet. I sighted an aircraft which was illuminated by search-lights at about five miles away and was approaching me from the starboard side. I climbed at full throttle in order to intercept and when I got within 1,000 yards from the enemy machine, I flashed my signal of the day to the guns below, which were firing at least a 1,000 yards to the rear and about 300 feet below the target. However, the anti-aircraft guns did not cease fire, but I had started my attack, which started in a stern chase, the enemy was then heading towards the coast and turning alternatively from port to starboard, presumably as an evasive tactic to escape the search-lights.

This movement however gave me an advantage as it enabled me to gain ground by turning inside his turns. When I was 500 yards to his rear and about 300 feet below him, I pulled my boost cut out control, turned on his starboard beam and positioned myself thereon slightly below at 400 yards distance. From this position I gradually closed into around 50 yards, when my gunner opened fire on my orders, firing about 600 rounds, which were seen by my gunner and myself to hit the enemy directly from tail to cockpit.

The aircraft turned over in a steep bank to starboard and fell headlong to earth, half on its back. During this violent manoeuvre, the German almost rammed me, after recovering from my breakaway, the enemy aircraft had fallen so low that it was out of the search-lights, out of sight and into the darkness.

Still carrying on with the patrol, I caught sight of another enemy aircraft approximately 3,000 feet above me and about five miles away straight ahead, heading south-east over Tunbridge Wells. I climbed to intercept trying to head it off, but when within 1,000 yards, I saw another aircraft, which I presumed to be the enemy to the rear of the first aeroplane. I climbed up until I was positioned 1,000 yards on the starboard beam of the leading aircraft, at this juncture I saw the following aircraft open fire with his front guns on the one in front.

I identified the pursing aircraft to be a friendly Bristol Blenheim fighter (I had not been informed of his presence in my vicinity). It is possible that the Blenheim hit the enemy aircraft in the tail, but the bomber was returning fire from its rear blister gun. Then the Blenheim appeared to cease fire, then broke away, I then decided to engage the enemy who was beginning to slip away. I got within 30 yards of him, when my gunner opened fire with a short burst which went over the top of the enemy aircraft; my gunner then corrected his aim and fired an 8-second burst from his guns. This set alight one of the engines and the plane appeared to dive down. I had overshot my mark and had placed myself slightly ahead of my enemy, who fired a short burst of incendiary bullets from his front gun which hit the turret. This caused me to breakaway to starboard.

> This aircraft was seen by the coastguard to be on fire, and the RDF (radar direction finding) ceased plotting it, eight miles from the French coast, where it obviously fell into the sea. Although no confirmation had been received, this enemy aircraft was only claimed as a 'probable,' as it had only one engine on fire. I respectfully beg to apply for a 'destroyed' verdict, as well as for the first action. Landed at 1.16 am.

The next evening, their success continued when a Junkers Ju88 Werke No. 2152 of 3/KG54 on a mission to bomb the London Docks was intercepted and attacked near Barking, Essex. The enemy aircraft turned for home, after being attacked it eventually fell to earth over Maidstone, with the main wreckage falling on St. Andrews Close and Tonbridge Road at 11.45 pm. The Defiant's crew were pilot Sergeant George Laurence and gunner Sergeant Wilfred Chard. The remainder of 'B' Flight was sent over to Gatwick to operate for the next day, where seven operational patrols were carried out.

Pilot Officer Tony Bartley of 92 Squadron remembers one particular sortie during the morning of 18th September 1940 at 9.45 am which took place near Appledore, south of Ashford, Kent:

> I remember one of the scariest of incidents that happened to me, was on 18th September, I had been having a pop at a Dornier bomber and I had forgotten one of the most crucial rules of air-fighting, which was always check behind. When suddenly a Messerschmitt 109 came down behind and shot me up very, very badly. I knew that my aeroplane was finished, so I undid my Sutton harness and prepared to jump over the side and use my parachute, when he came around at me again. I thought, if I bale out and he doesn't play the rules and opens fire, I'm dead, if he shoots me in my parachute. I thought the only way to do it is to get back in; and I took the controls and did a tight turn; because I always knew that the Spitfire could out turn a 109. I got inside him, but I could hardly see him, but I fired a burst of tracer and

> whether he thought he hadn't hit me as badly, he suddenly took off and by that time because of the action I was down to around 500 feet.
>
> At this height I couldn't jump and it was very risky. I therefore decided there was only one thing to do and this was to crash-land. So I headed for some marshland I had observed below, and decided to put my aircraft down there. As I had undone my straps previously, when I landed I was thrown out of the cockpit, landing completely unhurt in a ditch. I scrambled back to my Spitfire and when I lifted out my parachute, I found that it had been completely destroyed by a cannon shell and was literally in shreds. To think that I had nearly baled-out with this parachute, if the German had not turned in a second time, I would have baled-out and been killed with a useless parachute. So he saved my life.

The next day following his lucky escape, he penned a letter to his mother in which he wrote:

> Despite our losses the morale of the fighter boys is terrific. We will crack the German Air Force at all costs. This is our greatest and diciest hour, but we are proud to have a chance to deal with it. I am safe until my predestined time runs out. I am happy and almost enjoying myself. In these times of danger one gets drawn much closer to one's friends and a great spiritual feeling of comradeship and love envelops everyone. I can't explain, but everyone seems much better men somehow.

Tony Bartley continues:

> Just a few days later, my luck was in again, when during another encounter with the escort fighters, my aircraft was badly shot up. I told the controllers over the R/T that my flying controls were badly damaged, I could pull back the control stick and it worked, but if I moved it forward there was nothing.

> I was still at around 1,000 feet, but did not really want to take to my parachute, so I contacted the controller and he said 'if you can save the aircraft, do you think you can bring it in? I said I would try.
>
> I could work my aircraft on the trimming tab control. I trimmed the aircraft and was easing back on the stick, using the ailerons I brought it into Biggin Hill and did a perfect landing. I rolled to the end of the runway and as I pulled up and stopped, the cables on the control stick snapped, there was nothing left. But I was down; everything else had been shot away.

Two other pilots from 92 Squadron also received a mauling from the 109s; Pilot Officer Roy Mottram had no option but to vacate his burning Spitfire after receiving bullets that ignited his engine. He was slightly burned; he floated down, landed and was then taken to Orpington Hospital. His Spitfire N3193 crashed and burned at Hollingbourne. The other pilot was the New Zealander Flight Lieutenant James Paterson who had to crash-land his Spitfire K9991 at Debden during an afternoon sortie in which he was involved in combat against Heinkel bombers near the Essex coast.

No. 72 Squadron had also been in action that morning and had suffered from being bounced by high-flying Messerschmitt 109s who caught the squadron unaware. Sergeant Howard Bell-Walker was seriously wounded flying Spitfire R6704, as bullets ripped into his aircraft. He dived away and was able to land and receive treatment for his wounds spending many moths in hospital. Pilot Officer John Lloyd in Spitfire P9368 was also hit by the 109s and had to undertake a force-landing at Martin Mill, near Dover, he too was wounded seriously. Spitfire X4337 flown by Sergeant Norman Norfolk also managed to force-land his damaged aircraft at Hawkinge.

Two days later, on 20th, both 72 and 92 Squadrons were ordered to patrol over the Dungeness area of Kent, when radar picked up a large formation of enemy fighters heading inland towards London. Taking off from the aerodrome at 11.15, the squadrons climbed up to an altitude of 27,000 feet, at this height, whilst seeking out the enemy, they were bounced from above by Messerschmitt 109 of JG51 led by the German ace Werner Molders.

Diving through the formation of 92 Squadron, two Spitfires immediately dropped out of formation. This was Pilot Officer Howard Hill in Spitfire X4417 and Sergeant Peter Eyles flying N3248. Both men had been shot down by Molders.

Howard Hill, a New Zealander who hailed from Christchurch had joined the RAF in 1938, after completion of his flying training he had been posted to 92 Squadron then based at Tangmere in late October 1939. The squadron had been equipped with Bristol Blenheims; these were to be replaced by Spitfires in March 1940. Hill had three aircraft victories to his credit before the 20th. He had been flying in the rear section of the formation, when his aircraft was hit.

Following the Germans attack, it is claimed by pilots of 92 Squadron that they saw his aircraft heading in a westerly direction flying low over the treetops, thereafter no trace was seen of him. His Spitfire was found at West Hougham, between Dover and Folkestone with his burnt remains still in the cockpit, his body was recovered and laid to rest at Folkestone New Cemetery, Hawkinge. Peter Eyles from Basingstoke was never found, his Spitfire crashed into the sea off Dungeness. He is remembered on the Runnymede Memorial.

72 Squadron also suffered the loss of a pilot; this was Pilot Officer Denis 'Dutch' Holland. He had joined the squadron in early 1940, had also claimed a number of victories. He was shot down over Canterbury, Holland although badly wounded was able to climb out of his Spitfire X4410 and open his parachute. He was quickly taken to hospital, but succumbed to his injuries soon after arriving. His aircraft plummeted to earth at Stiff Street near Sittingbourne.

Squadron Leader Robert Lister was posted to 92 Squadron on 22nd September as a supernumerary and took over as commanding officer when Phillip Sanders had accidently set himself alight at dispersal. On 24th, he led 92 Squadron into battle and later recorded the mission:

We were scrambled soon after dawn and wasted no time forming a 'Big Wing' of three squadrons. We met the enemy head-on and below while still climbing – an impossible situation. They consisted of about nine Ju88s, surrounded by more than a hundred Me109s at various levels.

After breaking up the formation and avoiding any collision I found myself alone with nine or more 109s. In spite of a continued tight turn, one of them got me with a single cannon shell in the bottom of my cockpit between my legs, which were obviously wounded, also my left wrist. Instinctively after tight turns and spins, I blacked out. When I came to, I had come out of my spin, much lower down, the sky was completely empty.

On returning to Biggin Hill I lowered the flaps for landing. The Spitfire immediately went into a diving and skidding left-hand turn; I was unable to control it. After a few seconds I realised that only one flap had come down, so I raised the flap lever. Nevertheless, it seemed an age before the Spitfire answered. We went below the level of the airfield, down a valley which was fortunately there. A number of chicken houses flashed past my left wing as the Spitfire answered the controls; it seemed by a matter of only a few feet that I missed them and the ground.

On climbing up I realised that I would have to make a flapless landing, so I did a hurried circuit. By then I was feeling rather weak from the loss of blood and no doubt from some shock. I did not know what the correct approach speed should be without flaps, so came in on the slightly fast side. On touching down, I switched off the engine to reduce speed and applied the brakes as hard as I could. To my surprise, because I had fully expected to overshoot, I eventually came to rest intact, about twenty feet short of a wood at the end of the airfield. I was then carted off to Orpington Hospital and was off flying duties for about a year.

Lister was finally declared medically unfit for flying duties in June 1941, but returned to Biggin Hill to take up the position as a controller in the operations room. Post war, he later commanded RAF Wattisham and also RAF Newton before his retirement in 1954 at the rank of group captain.

From this encounter with the enemy, Pilot Officer John Bryson was killed in Spitfire X4037, crashing to earth near North Weald; and Sergeant William Ellis was forced to crash-land his Spitfire X4356 after he received damage to his starboard mainplane and glycol tank in fighting 109s over Maidstone.

After spending some time with his family on leave, he received a letter of his new posting to join No. 92 Squadron at RAF Biggin Hill; Sergeant Donald Kingaby travelled by train on 25th September and alighted at Bromley South Station. He then boarded the local bus to Leaves Green Village. He then walked the final part of his journey to the aerodrome.

On his arrival, he was dumb struck at the scene of the bombed buildings and debris caused by the Luftwaffe's attempts to knock out the aerodrome and its squadrons. No sooner had he taken in the devastation, when suddenly he became aware of the sound of an aircraft flying overhead. The aeroplane was a German Junkers Ju88; fortunately it dropped no bombs and once over the station headed south and back to France.

Kingaby had during this time, like everybody else, jumped for cover into the nearest slit trench or shelters. Once the threat had passed, he asked the way to the Sergeants' Mess and on arrival found this deserted. He waited around and was eventually shown by a flight sergeant, where he was to be billeted and to whom he would share a room. After meeting some of the other sergeant pilots and having a meal, he settled down for the night.

After a somewhat disturbed sleep caused by the local anti-aircraft gun-site firing off at intervals at night raiders, he was woken just before dawn and prepared himself for his first day with 92 Squadron. After a quick breakfast, he was taken down to the crew room at dispersal and here he met some of the other pilots he would fly with. After changing into his flying kit and picking up a parachute, he was then under the guidance of Flight Lieutenant Brian Kingcome, now an old hand with

92 Squadron.

He was shown the Spitfire he would be flying that day; after checking it with his ground crew, Kingaby returned to the dispersal room and sat down with the rest of the pilots and waited for the call to action. One of the other sergeant pilots was Ralph 'Titch' Havercroft, probably the smallest fighter pilot in Fighter Command at five foot three inches; his height did not restrict his fighting and flying ability in the air; he would sit on his parachute and place an extra cushion to be able to be comfortable in the cockpit and at the right height. He would become an ace.

The weather that day was not ideal, with heavy cloud. It was not until the afternoon that Green Section of 92 Squadron was called on to undertake a patrol. No enemy formations were sighted, but they did encounter separately three German aircraft, of which one was claimed as probably destroyed.

The next day, 27th September, was to be quite different however, with Radar picking up large plots of enemy formations during the early morning. At 9.05 am, both 92 and 72 Squadrons were ordered into the air and picked up a formation of twenty Dornier 17s with Me109 escort at 9.15 am near Sevenoaks.

Led by Brian Kingcome, he ordered 92 Squadron down into a diving attack against the bombers before the German fighters joined into the affray. A number of enemy aircraft were shot down, Kingcome claiming a Dornier destroyed and one damaged, while Sergeant Hugh Bowen-Morris and Pilot Officer Allan Wright damaged a further two, a Messerschmitt 110 was seen to be severely damaged by Pilot Officer 'Wimpy' Wade.

In return for their efforts the Germans shot down two of the squadron's aircraft, Spitfire R6767 in which Flight Sergeant Charles Sydney was killed, his aircraft crashing at Kingston-upon-Thames. Spitfire X4422 was being flown by New Zealander Flying Officer James Paterson. His aircraft was hit and set alight by 109s over Maidstone; Paterson was unable to extricate himself from his burning aircraft and was killed when it crashed at Sparepenny Lane, Farningham, Kent.

A memorial stone was unveiled at Sparepenny Lane on Wednesday 27th September 2006, this was organised and funded by the Shoreham Aircraft Museum, with members of Paterson's family in attendance coming all the way from New Zealand.

No. 72 Squadron had also been just as successful, having claimed six of the enemy destroyed with one probably destroyed and one damaged. They lost two pilots during this combat, Pilot Officer Ernest Males, just twenty years old from Southgate in London, he had been with the squadron since June 1940 and had three victories to his credit. He was shot down by 109s, his Spitfire crashed at Shadwell Dock, Stepney in East London. The other casualty was Flying Officer Paul Davies Cooke aged 23 from Shrewsbury; he was shot down over Bromley, his Spitfire N3068 fell on to houses No. 70 and 72 at the Queensway, West Wickham. He had baled-out, but his parachute failed to open and he fell to his death near Hayes Station

92 squadron was to suffer a third casualty later that day, that of 21 year old Sergeant Trevor Oldfield. During the morning, Oldfield had shot down a German fighter over Canterbury and claimed it destroyed as his final combat report states:

> I was Green 4, detailed to weave about above the squadron formation. When in the Canterbury area I was weaving approximately 1,000 feet above the squadron, when the squadron split up and engaged Me109s.
>
> Owing to my being above the squadron, I was able to turn sharply to the left and attacked a Me109 from quarter stern. I saw pieces fly off the enemy aircraft near the wing roots and after giving him a 3-second burst, I had only time to see him half roll and dive down, before I spun out. I could not see whether the aircraft crashed, but about 2-minutes later I saw someone making a parachute descent.

Sergeant Oldfield then took off in company with other pilots on a patrol that afternoon at 2.45 pm and intercepted a large bomber formation being escorted by an even larger fighter escort. The Spitfires attacked from head-on and had forced the bombers to split up. In doing so, each Spitfire then had individual combats with both bombers and fighters. Oldfield is believed to have been shot down by one of the overwhelming force of 109s as he broke away from an attack on the bombers.

His Spitfire crashed at Fullers House, Hesketh Park just outside of Dartford at 3.45 pm, close to the local Home Guard Headquarters, whose men immediately removed Oldfield's body from the wreckage. He was given a full military burial at St. Stephen's Church cemetery at Chertsey in Surrey. In 2007, a granite memorial was unveiled in his memory at Hesketh Park, provided once again by funds raised by the Shoreham Aircraft Museum.

Three other pilots from the squadron all received battle-damage of varying degrees that day. Pilot Officer Mansell-Lewis arrived back at base with a large section of his tailplane shot way in Spitfire X4480, Pilot Officer 'Wimpy' Wade had his aircraft P9544 damaged by enemy machine gun fire from a Dornier that he had been attacking over Brighton. He was obliged to force-land and in doing so, on landing at Macehill Lewes Race Course his Spitfire overturned, but Wade was uninjured. The third pilot, Sergeant Bowen-Morris also crash-landed back at Biggin following an afternoon combat in Spitfire R6760, and suffered no injury.

Don Kingaby recalls this period of hectic activity, and how continuous action and tiredness did become the norm for fighter pilots to endure; and memories waiting for the call to action:

> We had to be on from 4.00 am in the morning to about 10 o'clock at night. There were very few spare pilots around and sleep became quite a problem at night. I felt that at Biggin particularly, they had been fighting very hard and I felt I must keep fit, but I found this rather difficult because the billet we had been placed in was only fifty yards from the heavy ack-ack battery, which practically blew us out of bed every night. I tried taking aspirin and going down to the air-raid shelters for the night, the aspirins didn't work and

in the shelter you could hear everything just as much. I would wake with a foul mouth in the morning and feel absolutely washed out. After about four days of this, I just joined the other chaps in the bar, had a few pints of beer, after which I was able to sleep contentedly.

The next morning I would arrive down at the dispersal hut in the gloom of the pre-dawn period, collect my kit, parachute and helmet and take them over to my aircraft, the one I had been allotted. I would then hang the helmet over the control stick and check around the cockpit and make sure everything was ready for a quick getaway.

Back at the dispersal hut we played cards, pontoon, and poker or just read a book and play gramophone records. We had a couple of pilots who were great 'Jazz' enthusiasts, 'Titch' Havercroft and Bob Holland. We had an old piano there and they use to jive around on.

There was a telephone line from the sector operations room direct to our hut and as soon as a message came through on that, the clerk would yell out 'scramble.' Bells would begin to ring and flares would sometimes be fired, then there would be a mad rush out of the door, as every pilot would do his damnedness to get to his aeroplane as quick as possible.

We would then form up as a squadron of twelve if available; then all take off in formation together. It could be a bit hazardous at times, if the leader slightly misjudged his throttle handling, because usually at Biggin you had to avoid obstructions or where bomb holes had sometimes not been completely filled in.

Once you were airborne, it would very as to the time we made contact with the enemy, depending on the type of raid and the tactics that the fighter controller back in the sector ops room was using. During September, we were mainly intercepting bombers flying at 17,000 to 20,000 feet, heavily escorted by fighters. The controllers would try to divert us away from the bombers first, and then bring us back into them from behind the sun and from above, if they could, to give us the advantage.

92 Squadron flew again on the 29th September, when Green Section led by Pilot Officer Williams carried out a patrol between Maidstone and Canterbury at 3.00 pm; He sighted a lone Dornier 17 about a mile in front of him, flying just above the clouds. He carried out an attack and saw his tracer bullets enter the middle section of the bomber, which then went into a spiral dive and entered cloud. He could not confirm whether the German had crashed, but the ground controller reported that the radar plot had disappeared at Canterbury.

On the last day of September, whilst on patrol at 5.00pm, Pilot Officer Allan Wright of 92 Squadron in Spitfire X4069 had to undertake a forced-landing at Shoreham-on-Sea, East Sussex, after being wounded after he was attacked by a Messerschmitt 109. His aircraft was written-off, but he survived to fight another day.

# Chapter 7
# October
# 1940

By the beginning of October, the Luftwaffe High Command had more or less come to the conclusion that any chance of knocking out the Royal Air Force had now gone and that an invasion of south-east England would be out of the question. New tactics were to be employed to bring Britain to her knees. Bombing raids against London during the daylight hours were phased out and now would be undertaken at night. Never again would the Luftwaffe send mass raids, which had caused them so many casualties during September.

The new tactics now included fighter-bomber sweeps consisting of Messerschmitt Bf 109s and Messerschmitt Bf 110s. The 109s could carry a single 250 kilogram bomb, the Bf110s could carry six bombs, two 250 kilogram and four 50 kilogram devices. Although the bomb loads were small, the fighters had the advantage of speed and surprise and could fly in low if required to avoid Radar detection along the coast. The sweeps could be large or small, in formations or as single pairs of aircraft. The fast speed of the fighters would allow them to reach London within 35-minutes from take-off.

The first Luftwaffe raid using this new approach was tried on Tuesday 1st October 1940, when several formations of fifty to one hundred fighter-bombers swept over the Channel during the early morning at 7.00 am until late afternoon. Their targets were Portsmouth, Southampton and London. Strangely the German formations did not come in low, but at high level altitude of 25,000 feet. They were detected by Radar and British fighters were scrambled to intercept. The RAF fighters were vectored on to the interception expecting to have to cope with standard German bombers as they had previously. Climbing up to meet what they believed to be bombers with fighter protection, they were now confronted with just fighters, which was a completely new experience for some RAF pilots. Once again the RAF fighters were at a height disadvantage, having not been sent off earlier to gain height in time to meet the approaching Germans.

Weather conditions were also not favourable as it was a mainly cloudy day and British fighters had difficulty in finding their foe; who were sometimes hidden in cloud. Combat was met and both sides sustained casualties, the RAF losses amounted to five aircraft, four Hurricanes and one Spitfire; with three pilots killed, the Germans losing two Bf109s with one pilot killed, the other becoming a prisoner of war and a Bf110 with the loss of both crewmen.

This new threat was now subject of urgent discussion among the Fighter Command leaders, Hugh Dowding and Keith Park of 11 Group. It was decided that to allow the squadrons time to get airborne and be adequately positioned to counter the German fighter sweeps, that 'standing patrols' be organised between the various aerodromes in the south-east. Patrol lines at a height of 15,000 feet were set and sections of fighters flying at cruising speed could scan the sky for intruders and relay back information as soon as the enemy was detected. They could then meet the threat in a good position to attack.

Air Vice-Marshal Keith Park's instructions which were issued to his operational controllers and commanders gave an outline to the countermeasures that he envisaged using against the Luftwaffe at this time.

> Because of the lack of height reports, the delays from the RDF and Observer Corps information at Group, it takes longer time recently taken by squadrons to take off, pairs and wings of squadrons were meeting the enemy formation above them, before reaching the height ordered by Group.
>
> Tip and run raids across Kent by Bf110s carrying bombs or small formations of long-range bombers escorted by fighters, give such short notice that the Group controller is sometimes compelled

> to detail single fighter squadrons that happen to be in the air to intercept enemy bombers before they attacked aircraft factories, sector aerodromes or other vital targets, such as docks, Woolwich etc.
>
> Occasionally, reconnaissance Spitfires or Hurricanes from Hornchurch or Biggin Hill are able to sight and report the height and particulars of enemy formations. Moreover, a special fighter reconnaissance flight is now being formed at Gravesend for the purpose of getting information about approaching enemy raids.
>
> Whenever time permits, I wish Group controllers to get the 'readiness' squadron in company over sector aerodromes, Spitfires at 25,000 feet and Hurricanes at 20,000 feet, and wait until they report or are in a good position before sending them to patrol lines to intercept raids, having a good track in fairly clear weather.

On 2nd October, Squadron Leader Alan Moncrieff MacLachlan arrived at Biggin Hill and took over command of No. 92 Squadron; and the pilots were moved to sleeping quarters outside the aerodrome at Southwood, two-miles from Biggin Hill. This was a beautiful country house owned by Captain McNair-Scott. Tony Bartley remembers:

> The bombing got so bad after a while that we were not allowed to live on the base, so we were moved into temporary accommodation which was an old army mess, a sort of prefab. Then Fighter Command became so nervous that there were three squadrons on the airfield that they said we couldn't live on the airfield at night, they then billeted us in country houses two to three miles from the airfield. 72 Squadron went to one place and we went to another and the third squadron somewhere else. They were afraid that if we lived in the officers' mess or the sergeants' mess, that one bomb would knock out the pilots of three squadrons.

On this day, the village of Biggin Hill witnessed an unexpected incident at around 10.00 am, when a Messerschmitt 109 fighter Werke No.

5374 of 8/JG53 fell from the sky following combat and crashed at Sutherland Avenue. Its pilot Oberleutnant Siegfried Stronk was killed. Around the same time another 109 of Stab III/JG53 was shot down in combat over Biggin Hill and was claimed by two pilots, Pilot Officer John Kendal of 66 Squadron and Flying Officer Peter Dexter of No. 603 Squadron. The Messerschmitts pilot, Oberleutnant Walter Radlick took to his parachute, but it failed to open and he fell to his death at Hookwood Park near Limpsfield. His aircraft came down next to New Road, Limpsfield Common near Oxted.

Immediately after shooting at Radlicks 109, Peter Dexter was himself shot down and suffered a bullet wound to one of his legs, as he attempted to vacate his Spitfire P9553; one leg became trapped. Having falling 15,000 feet, he eventually managed to break free, leaving one of his flying boots behind. He was still at a reasonable height for his parachute to deploy fully and on landing at Featherbed Lane, Addington, was taken to Croydon Hospital, where he received treatment for his wound. His Spitfire came down at Castle Hill Farm, Addington.

No. 72 Squadron lost one of its pilots in a mid-air collision soon after taking off from the aerodrome at 9.45 am on October 5th after the squadron was given instructions to patrol Maidstone. Pilot Officer Norman Sutton aged 26, from St. Helen's Lancashire, was flying in Spitfire K9989 when he collided with Sergeant Robert Staples in Spitfire X4454. Sutton was killed in the collision, but Staples managed to land back at the aerodrome without injury.

There was great rejoicing within 92 Squadron on 9th October, when news arrived that Flight Lieutenant Brian Kingcome and Pilot Officer Tony Bartley had each been awarded the Distinguished Flying Cross. That evening the pilots drove up to the White Hart at Brasted and celebrated into the early hours.

Not so good news was the loss earlier that day of Sergeant Eric Frith aged 20, who was shot down by a Messerschmitt 109. He managed to parachute down from his doomed aircraft X4597, but was very badly burned. On landing, he was quickly admitted to the Willesborough Hospital, but succumbed to his injuries on 17th October. His Spitfire crashed at The Ridgeway, Smeeth, near Ashford.

Flying Officer Robert Hugh Holland of 92 Squadron, in a letter to WAAF Section Officer 'Bunty' Nash on 10th October wrote about the squadron's new accommodation and some of the pilots in his squadron:

My Dear Bunty

Well I returned some days ago and we are still at it all day and every day, my God, the peace of Pembury after this place would be heaven. However, we have a marvellous time in the evenings here as we are living in a wizard billet, which is a large family house we have taken over, with a dance floor, piano, drums double bass and plenty of volunteer musicians to go with them.

We have a night club there every night, our drink bill is mounting up something terrific; but still what the hell!

Poor old Bill Williams and Drummond were killed this morning, they must move us soon for a rest. Tony Bartley, Allan Wright who is in hospital, and myself are the only original members of the squadron left, from when it was formed. That was a year ago today, so we are having an anniversary party tonight. By the way did you know that Allan Wright, Brian Kingcome and Tony Bartley all have DFC's now? Tucky came down to see us yesterday, he has got a bar to his DFC and has now shot down 19-Huns!

Our new CO is an absolute wizard and thrashes like nobody's business. Well I must go and eat now.

Much love, Bob

No. 92 Squadron suffered the loss of two of its pilots on 10th October, when at 8.30 am, Pilot Officer John Fraser Drummond aged 21 and Pilot Officer Desmond Gordon Williams aged 20, were in the process of attacking a Dornier 17 bomber over Tangmere in West Sussex, when their two Spitfires collided. Williams's aircraft X4038 crashing east of Brighton and Drummonds Spitfire R6616 crashing and burning out at Jubilee Fields, Portslade. Drummond was seen to bale-out and was wounded in an arm and leg, but was too low for his parachute to deploy.

Pilot Officer Peter Pool whilst on patrol with a section of 72 Squadron, giving air cover to a convoy off the coast of Deal; became engaged with Messerschmitt 109s and his aircraft, Spitfire K9870 was hit by bullets and cannon fire. Pool was wounded, his aircraft burst into flames, but he managed to open the cockpit hatch and baled-out. He landed safely, his Spitfire crashing at Milton Regis, Sittingbourne at 8.00pm

On the morning of 12th October, 92 Squadron was ordered off and met the enemy; during an interception Squadron Leader Robert Stanford Tuck who had been invited up, was able to claim his twentieth victory.

Whilst on patrol during that morning, No. 72 Squadron lost Pilot Officer Herbert Case, when his Spitfire P9338 suddenly dropped out of formation. Possibly Case became the victim of oxygen failure and passed out, but he was killed when his aircraft plunged into the ground at Capel-le-Ferne near Folkestone at 9.20 am.

During the afternoon, the 92 Squadron was scrambled again and achieved further success, when another three enemy aircraft were destroyed, claimed by Flight Lieutenant Brian Kingcome, Pilot Officer 'Wimpy' Wade and Sergeant Don Kingaby. Sadly the action claimed the life of Pilot Officer Aberconway Pattinson, shot down on his first patrol in Spitfire X4591; it crashed and burnt out in Bartholomew's Wood, Postling Wents north of Hythe.

Brian Kingcome was leading the squadron on 15th October, when they were scrambled during that morning. The squadron was heavily involved in action with enemy fighters over the Thames Estuary 10.00 am, during this engagement they lost Sergeant Kenneth Parker, whose Spitfire R6838 dived into the water off Hoo Marina in Medway Estuary. His body eventually was recovered some time later off the Dutch coast and he was buried in the Terschelling General Cemetery.

Kingcome led the squadron once again on another patrol at 11.00 am. It was a morning that he would always remember:

We had taken off from Biggin at around 11.00 am; the usual thing, x-number of aircraft approaching from wherever with fighter escort. There was about six or eight of us; I did my usual thing of flying like crazy northwards before turning to intercept them over Maidstone. Then it was everyman for himself with the sky full of turning and weaving aeroplanes in a general melee, before suddenly the sky appeared empty. I looked around and it was a beautiful day and I could see Biggin Hill in the distance and I was at about 25,000 feet and then I did an absurd thing. I decided to try practicing a force-landing. So I throttled back and started to glide, but my mind was focused on the eggs and bacon I hoped to get once I had landed back at the aerodrome.

The next moment there was the rattle and bang, something hit my leg and I looked round quickly and there was three Spitfires drawing up alongside me who then half-rolled away. My Spitfire was in a bit of a state damage wise and I could see blood coming out of my flying boot. I thought I better get down quick before I ended up bleeding to death; being shot does not hurt at the time, it just felt like somebody had given me a thump. I decided to bale-out, this was at an altitude of about 10,000 feet. I pulled my chute and just gently floated down; I could see people gathering underneath me. I thought 'Oh no' because I was wearing a Mae West preserver I had taken from a German pilot I had shot down in Wales.

There had been many occasions in those days when people had beaten up RAF pilots thinking they were Germans. One or two of them had pitch forks and I thought this is not good. Anyway it turned out alright for me. They asked me what hospital I wanted to be taken too, I said 'What have you got,' they said there was a naval hospital at Chatham. I thought that should be alright, they must know about bullet wounds there. But they made a balls up of it, the surgeon all most killed me by instead of looking for the bullet, first using x-ray, he started cutting into my leg probing for it and cutting a blood vessel, and finally tried to stop the bleeding by filling the wound with gauze and plaster wrap and crossing his fingers.

Whether the Spitfires had shot me down or they had shot a German off my tail, I never did find out.

Kingcome spent the next six weeks recovering from his wound, and then he returned to the squadron. His Spitfire X4418 had crashed at Wyborne's Farm, High Halstow.

Also on the receiving end, was Pilot Officer John Lund in Spitfire R6642. During the combat with the 109s, his aircraft was shot down and he took to his parachute and landed in the sea. He was fortunately rescued by the naval vessel HMS *Nysan*. His aircraft crashed into the water off Bee Ness Jetty.

On 16th October No. 72 Squadron left Biggin and were replaced by No. 74 'Tiger' Squadron who had been operating from RAF Coltishall in Norfolk as part of No. 12 Group. Led by the charismatic South African Adolph 'Sailor' Malan who was an extremely experienced fighter leader with a high score of enemy aircraft destroyed to match,; they also had many exceptional pilots within their ranks, such as John Mungo-Park, Harbourne Mackay Stephen, John Freeborn and the Polish flyer Henryk Szczesny. Their radio call-sign was 'Dysoe.'

The next day, the squadron carried on notching up more German aircraft when at 3.10 pm, eleven aircraft took off after receiving instructions to carry out a patrol. After a short while they were notified over the radio that a large force of enemy aircraft was approaching London from the south. They sighted anti-aircraft shells bursting over the Thames Estuary and sighted a formation of around 60 plus Messerschmitt 109s flying north. They headed towards the formation as quickly as possible and intercepted the enemy fighters over the Maidstone and Gravesend area. Malan positioned his men up sun of the Germans and gave the order to attack with the usual cry of 'Tally Ho.' Soon each man was caught up in individual combat.

Malan picked out one of the 109s and gave it a two-second burst from 200-yards, then another as he got within 150-yards. He was now down to 100-yards from his opponent when he delivered a final burst of fire, which damaged the elevator control of the 109, which sent it into a vertical dive, as black smoke began to pour from the machine. Malan was unable to follow his victim down as he himself 'blacked-out for a couple of seconds due to the severe G-Forces caused by the manoeuvring of his Spitfire.

Pilot Officer Brian Draper had attacked one of seven 109s which were flying in line astern ahead and slightly below. He fired a burst at one of the enemy fighter and saw it go down in flames. Pilot Officer Peter St. John was also able to claim one of the enemy fighters after firing from 250 yards range, he saw the 109 roll over on to its back and fall away in a dive with flames licking from its engine. As the Spitfires began landing back at Biggin between 4.15 and 4.30 pm, the pilots had given their reports to the squadron intelligence officer; they claimed to have destroyed three 109s and two probably destroyed.

Unfortunately one of the Spitfires failed to return from the encounter; this was Spitfire P7360 which was being flown by Flying Officer Alan Leslie Ricalton aged 26 years who originated from Hazelrigg in Northumberland. His aircraft had been seen to fall away during the combat and was later found crashed near Hollingbourne, Kent. His body was laid to rest at Sittingbourne Cemetery.

Sergeant Pilot Leslie Alton of 92 Squadron was killed on 19th October while flying Spitfire R6922; the circumstances of his death were never satisfactorily explained. It is thought that he may have suffered from oxygen failure or that he was the victim of a surprise attack. He came from Nuneaton and was an excellent sportsman; having captained the football, cricket and hockey teams at the King George VI Grammar School which he had attended. He had previously served with No. 266 Squadron before being posted to No. 92 in September 1940. His aircraft crashed on Tuesnoad Farm at Smarden.

74 were again in action during the afternoon at 2.00 pm on 20th, when they along with No. 66 Squadron from Gravesend were instructed to patrol Biggin at 30,000 feet. Over Maidstone they sighted over thirty Messerschmitt 109s approaching from the south just 1,000 feet

below them. On seeing the RAF machines, the German fighters broke formation; some of them were seen to dive, while others were half climbing. The pilots of 74 Squadron then began to pick individual aircraft to attack. Flight Lieutenant John Mungo-Park attacked one of the last aircraft in the enemy formation as it began to climb and fired at it from 100-yards range, it immediately started to spin and following it down to 4,000 feet, he observed the Germans tail-section fall away.

Pilot Officer Stephen attacked four of the 109s who promptly dived away in the direction of Dungeness. He followed them and singled out one firing from 500 yards and witnessed the tail start to break up, and then the top of the cockpit canopy flew off. He then had to break away as three 109s were trying to get above him. In the action that followed, he was able to fire his guns into another German machine and saw the pilot bale-out, before the aircraft crash into a wood.

Pilot Officer Brian Draper attacked a single 109 which had turned north over the Thames and then had tried to return south. He fired a burst from his machine guns from astern of the enemy aircraft, but was in return hit by an unseen German fighter, which punctured his oil radiator and he was forced to crash-land. On the way down he saw an enemy aircraft obviously out of control and considered that if it did crash it would be in the Kidbrooke- Woolwich area.

Later that afternoon he received information from the station intelligence officer at Biggin Hill that a 109 had been reported to have crashed at Woolwich confirming Draper's claim.

Sergeant Brian Kirk was reported to have shot down a Messerschmitt and had seen large pieces of fuselage and a wing fall off, before he was shot down himself. Kirk was very badly wounded during the encounter and baled-out of his Spitfire P7360 which crashed at Coxheath. Kirk was rushed to Preston Hall Hospital, but died of his wounds nine months later on 22nd July 1941.

Also wounded that day was Sergeant Clive Hilken, who had baled-out of his Spitfire during combat with fighters over South London at 3.00 pm. His Spitfire P7426 crashed at Cowden, Kent. Hilken on landing was admitted to Orpington Hospital.

Two days later on 22nd, both 74 and 92 Squadrons carried out a joint patrol over Maidstone at 1.50 pm that afternoon. The squadrons were given various courses to locate bomb-carrying Messerschmitt 109s who were flying in across the coast to bomb targets of opportunity. Flying at 30,000 feet they sighted several 109s steering south-east over Ashford at 28,000 feet. 92 Squadron cried 'Tally Ho' and dived into the attack with 74. 'Sailor' Malan and Mungo-Park each claimed one of the 109s, but Flying Officer Peter St. John was killed in the combat. His Spitfire P7431, crashing at South Nutfield, near Redhill, Surrey.

Pilot Officer Robert Spurdle, a New Zealander was the only other casualty, he baled out of his aircraft P7364 over Tonbridge. He had been following a Me109, when suddenly his Spitfire flicked into a spin and he lost control. Peering to his starboard side, he was shocked to see a large space where the wing should have been. He immediately struggled to get out, but something was holding him back. As he frantically tried to open his cockpit canopy, his hands were cut and bleeding from the broken Perspex.

Realising he was still strapped in by his Sutton Harness; he pulled out the holding pin and tore away his radio cable from his flying helmet. He was suddenly blown out by the centrifugal force and the next second he reached for the D-Ring of his parachute, pulled it and felt the tremendous jerk as the silk canopy opened. It took him another twenty minutes to float from 20,000 feet, before he landed in a field at Tonbridge that was filled with hop-pickers who had witnessed his decent. He was whisked away by the local police bobby and waited at a local house to be picked up by car and taken back to Biggin Hill. In the meantime he was given tea and cake. His Spitfire crashed at Hadlow Place, near Tonbridge. Once back at the aerodrome and being checked over by the medical officer, he was given five days leave in London. No. 92 failed to claim any enemy machines that day.

The weather during the morning of the 25th October was bright and clear; several patrols were conducted, 92 Squadron was able to claim two 109s destroyed and one probable by Flight Lieutenant Villa and Pilot Officer Sherrington. The next day the weather remained dull with very low cloud and the squadrons remained on 'readiness.'

The next day, on 26th, 92 Squadron received their new commanding officer, Squadron Leader Johnny Kent. Kent was an experienced battle hardened pilot who had been born in Winnipeg, Canada and had learnt to fly and gained his license in 1931, before joining the Royal Air Force on a short service commission in 1935. In 1940, he had been posted to the Photographic Development Unit at Heston, and during the last days of the Battle of France had flown unarmed Spitfires; but he was sent to No. 7 Operational Training Unit at Hawarden in July 1940 to convert on to Hurricane fighters.

On 2nd August 1940, he was posted as a flight commander to join No. 303 (Polish) Squadron based at Northolt during which time he claimed several enemy aircraft and had helped to turn the squadron into one of the highest scoring squadrons in Fighter Command. The day before he moved to Biggin Hill, he had been awarded the Distinguished Flying Cross. The citation of his award stated the following:

> Early in October 1940, this officer when entirely alone attacked 40 Messerschmitt's and shot down two of them. He has personally destroyed at least four enemy aircraft. Flight Lieutenant Kent has been responsible in a large measure for the fighting efficiency of his squadron (303) and has materially contributed to its successes. He has proved himself a born leader.

Kent arrived at his new posting at around tea time and was shown to the officers' mess, where some of 92 Squadron's pilots were sitting down. He introduced himself to the officers and was not impressed with their lackadaisical approach. In later years he wrote about this first meeting:

> My first impressions were not favourable and their general lack of manners indicated a lack of control and discipline. I realised I was going to have my hands full.

Kent was already aware that the squadron had distinguished themselves in the air with scoring a high number of enemy aircraft destroyed, had also suffered many casualties and this was becoming a problem. 92 Squadron should have and was ready to be moved out of the fighting line for a rest period; Johnny Kent pulled no punches and speaking to higher officials in Fighter Command, suggested that the squadron would be better served and knocked back into shape if he were allowed to keep them at Biggin and work hard to get them even more efficient than before. Kent summoned the senior officers of 92 Squadron and began to put his plan into effect; these included the scaling down of the evening parties that were a regular feature at the Southwood House with all guests leaving by 11.00 pm. To be no irregularities as far as the wearing of uniform dress is concerned and the taking of aviation fuel to run their cars was to cease. Kent later commented on what he had requested:

> This action made me even more unpopular, but it eventually began to take effect on them all, when they became more efficient and happier. I was an unpleasant bastard, but I did it for their own good. I asked Tony Bartley to help me in the process and win over their co-operation, fortunately he agreed. Joining them some evenings at the White Hart pub also helped to cement the relationship.

74 Squadron met the enemy over Maidstone on 27th, when they engaged a formation of 109s at 9.00 am that morning. Leading the squadron was 'Sailor' Malan who following the combat was obliged to force-land his aircraft P7368 at Kenley due to battle damage. Pilot Officer Peter Chesters claimed a Messerschmitt 109E-4 (3525) of 3/JG52 and damaged it, causing its pilot Feldwebel Schieverhofer to force-land at the Penshurst landing ground. Chesters followed the 109 and landed beside it as Schieverhofer stepped out and was captured.

Sergeant Bill Skinner was also able to claim a 109, when he shot down Oberleutnant Ulrich Steinhilper. He parachuted down and landed with an injured leg. He was immediately captured and was sent to Canada as a prisoner of war and tried many unsuccessful escapes whilst there. His aircraft crashed at Upstreet near Canterbury. This aircraft was excavated by the Kent Battle of Britain Museum on 26th October 1980 and Steinhilper returned to view the remains of his aircraft soon after. It is now on show within the museum at Hawkinge.

The squadron's only casualty was Sergeant John Scott who had served previously with 266 and 611 Squadrons. His Spitfire P7526 crashed and exploded at Dundas Farm, Stowting, Kent, killing its pilot.

During the last few days of October, the weather drew in and clouded over, so no flying was undertaken. It was not until 29th that the weather resumed to bright and clear skies. 92 Squadron participated in several sorties during the morning, but two of their Spitfires piloted by Sergeants Bowen-Morris and Kingaby were damaged due to a taxing accident. During the afternoon, the squadron took to the air once again and met the enemy; several Messerschmitt 110s were engaged and three were shot down, one each by Flight Lieutenant Villa, Pilot Officer Saunders and Sergeant Bowen- Morris. The squadron suffered no casualties to themselves. This final sortie ended the flying operations for October at Biggin Hill as gale force winds restricted the Luftwaffe from mounting any further raids.

# Chapter 8
# November - December 1940

It was during this month, that construction teams moved on to the aerodrome, to at last undertake the large task of rebuilding or repairing the buildings and facilities that had been destroyed or damaged over the last two months from the raids by the Luftwaffe in trying to knock out Biggin Hill. As winter approached the conditions on the station were far from ideal and hastily constructed buildings leaked and mud ruled the site.

No. 74 Squadron was active during the first day of November and was involved in combat with German fighters over Dover, losing one of their most experienced pilots Flying Officer William Nelson, shot down in Spitfire P7312 in a surprise attack. His aircraft crashed into the Channel and his body was never recovered. Nelson had originally been a bomber pilot at the start of the war flying Avro Whitleys and had been awarded a Distinguished Flying Cross for his services by June 1940. He then volunteered to join Fighter Command and after training was sent to No. 74 Squadron on 20th July, then operating from RAF Hornchurch. During this period, he had claimed several enemy aircraft destroyed or damaged.

He had married in the August of 1939 and his wife Marjorie gives her memories of him:

> My husband 'Willie' came from Montreal, Canada in 1936 to join the RAF. I met him in 1939. He was stationed at Disforth at that time with No. 10 Bomber Squadron. We were married on 24th August before war was declared, then followed the 'Phoney War' when leaflets were dropped over Germany- I still have some of

them. Willie piloted a Whitley bomber with a maximum speed of 180 mph! I think now we must have been very innocent to suppose the leaflets would have much effect, and they were quickly followed by the bombings.

They were anxious times, but he had a very inspiring group captain as a commanding officer, who later appeared in a movie called 'Target for Tonight' and his wife Norah was a wonderful woman, who really looked after the wives of the air crews.

Willie was awarded the DFC in the spring of 1940, when invasion seemed imminent. He fought hard to join a Spitfire Squadron and was eventually transferred to the stations in the south-east at Hornchurch and finally Biggin Hill.

On August 30th, our much longed for baby son arrived and Willie managed to get compassionate leave to come north to Cotterstone to see us. He was very tired as he had been on operations since the beginning; I think that was the first time that 'battle fatigue' come into use. He was ordered to take two weeks leave, but fretting over the number of ill-trained pilots entering the war, he refused his leave. Returning to Biggin Hill, he was himself shot down on November 1st. A year later, I took my baby over to Canada hoping to start a new life. The pension for a flying officer's widow then was £10 per month.

Biggin Hill's only other casualty that day was Sergeant Harold Soars of 74 Squadron, who was wounded during combat with Messerschmitt 109s at 2.00 pm. He baled out of his Spitfire P7523 which crashed at Biggin Hill.

On 2nd November, four of Biggin Hill's WAAF personnel made their way up to London to receive their gallantry awards from His Majesty King George VI at Buckingham Palace for their courageous actions during the August raids upon the aerodrome. Section Officer Hanbury was awarded the MBE, Sergeant Elizabeth Mortimer, Sergeant Helen Turner and Corporal Elspeth Henderson each receiving the Military Medal. Also receiving an award was a civilian doctor A.M. Cole, he was awarded an OBE, for attending and assisting in the rescue of Pilot Officer Pfeiffer from 32 Squadron who had force-landed his aircraft at the aerodrome on 6th August.

That morning 92 Squadron had been ordered at 9.00 am to patrol over the aerodrome with 74 Squadron at 15,000 feet, after a few minutes they were then told to climb to an altitude of 30,000 feet. At this height the two squadrons began to give out the tell-tale vapour trails that could be picked up by any enemy aircraft flying in that vicinity, so Squadron Leader Johnny Kent descended his aircraft and that of 74 Squadron to a lower level. His report of that flight states the following:

> Shortly after attaining this height, we were instructed to patrol Maidstone. Upon arriving there we were vectored about a bit and advised that a large force of enemy aircraft was approaching from the south-east and would cross a line joining Maidstone and Tonbridge. We turned and I noticed anti-aircraft fire on our left. On turning towards it I saw a large force of Me109s below us at about 20,000 feet and I immediately led the squadron into attack.
>
> I approached behind one of the 109s to about 100 yards and opened fire. It immediately began to smoke furiously and dived steeply towards the ground. I watched it for some time and it crashed near a town which I think was Ashford.. I managed then to get behind another 109 and opened fire. I knocked pieces off it and it began to smoke heavily as it dived away. I did not see what happened to it as another 109 appeared behind me; I evaded this one and got on the tail of another, who flew very well and our dogfight lasted several minutes. He very cleverly used the sun by turning inland down sun and then out to sea.
>
> I managed however to get one or two good deflection shots in and he turned inland once more. I fired again from the beam and he turned on to his back and went down smoking and crashed at Dymchurch, about a quarter of a mile from the sea. A number of soldiers ran out to the wreckage, which was strewn over a good area and the main

part of the aircraft had completely buried itself as far as I could see.

Kent's victim had been Hauptmann Ensslen, the Gruppenkommandeur of Stab II/JG52; he had baled-out, but fell to his death. His aircraft Messerschmitt Bf109E-7 Werke No. 3784 crashed 200 yards east of Burmarsh Halt near Dymchurch. His identity at first could not be established as he carried no personal effects, the only clue was the shoulder insignia, that of a Hauptmann. It was only after interrogation of other captured pilots that his identity was confirmed.

During a patrol covering Biggin Hill on 6th November, No. 615 Squadron who was operating out of RAF Northolt lost one of its Hurricanes. Sergeant Jack Hammerton aged 25, was seen to break away from the formation at 25,000 feet, apparently having sighted an enemy aircraft. He failed to return, his Hurricane V323 was later found to have dived into the ground with great force near the railway line at Noah's Ark, near Sevenoaks. It is thought that he probably suffered from oxygen failure and had lost consciousness. His remains were recovered and he was buried in Stoke Road Cemetery at Slough.

No. 66 Squadron moved their Spitfires into Biggin Hill from West Malling on 7th November, due to their aerodrome becoming water-logged owing to torrential rain over the last four days. Their radio-call-sign was 'Fibus.'

The aerodrome was paid a visit by the Luftwaffe on the night of 10th November, when several bombs were dropped hitting a number of dispersal pens causing one aircraft of 92 Squadron to be burnt out, making three other Spitfires unserviceable. Two aircraft from No. 66 Squadron were also destroyed, plus five others damaged due to bomb splinters. There were no personnel casualties.

During the afternoon of the 14th, both 66 Squadron and No. 74 were scrambled at 2.15 pm, when an enemy raid was plotted heading towards the Dover area. Leading 66 Squadron on this sortie was Flight Lieutenant George Christie, a Canadian who had joined the RAF on a short term commission in 1937, he had flown with Douglas Bader's 242 Squadron during July and August of that year; he was posted to 66 Squadron on 3rd September. As the squadron approached the area between Deal and Dover, they sighted a formation of 40 Junkers Ju87 Stuka dive-bombers escorted by a larger formation of Messerschmitt 109s and 110s.

Christie ordered one section to take on the fighters, but as he did, he noticed a line of anti-aircraft shells exploding over the estuary. He noted that the 109s had now climbed higher to avoid the ground fire and followed them despite the risk of being hit by our own defences. As the 109s were to far ahead, he swung around and led the squadron around behind the Stukas and brought the squadron into attack from a starboard position. Meanwhile, 74 Squadron began their attack from port. Christie claimed a couple of Stukas himself as his combat report verifies:

> I carried out two attacks without visual damage, then I did an attack on a Stuka who turned over on its back and went straight down with petrol and glycol streaming from it.
>
> I had to roll to pass under the leading Ju87 in the formation, his gunner got a burst into my machine, this Ju87 went straight down as I avoided the leader, I looked down in time to see two Ju87s hit the water just off the mole at Dover; I think one of them was mine.
>
> My machine was still OK, so I got into a position for another attack on the 87s, but saw a Me109 above and ahead of me, so I attacked him. I got two bursts into him and he dived away with smoke pouring from his engine, but as I was attacked by three 109s I rolled over and went down. I saw another Ju87 by himself and made two attacks which finally sent him down in flames, he also crashed into the sea about four miles east of Dover.

On return back to base 66 Squadron put in claims for five Junkers Ju87s damaged, two destroyed and one probably destroyed, also one Messerschmitt 109 destroyed, one probably destroyed and one damaged. It had been a very successful engagement. No. 74 Squadron also had claimed a good number of the enemy; twelve Ju87s destroyed, 3 probably destroyed and one 109 destroyed. Pilot Officer Harbourne Mackay Stephen DFC claiming three Ju87s destroyed himself. Pilot Officer William Armstrong in Spitfire P7386 was shot down during combat, but he landed safely.

The squadrons also reported that the anti-aircraft battery positioned on the Isle of Sheppey fired continuously causing the squadrons to split up. The commander of 74 Squadron had complained over his radio, but the batteries refused to cease fire.

15th November, was another splendid day for 92 Squadron in regards to success against the Germans. Two patrols were flown that day and Sergeant Don Kingaby later talked about his success against the enemy in a wartime radio interview:

> The reason I've got so many Messerschmitt's maybe is because it was just my luck to have run into more of these enemy machines than any other type. The day I shot down four of them was when they were coming in over the Channel in droves. We don't see them like that at present, just the odd ones and two's dodging about in the cloud.
>
> On 15th November 1940, our squadron of Spitfires was sent out during the morning and intercepted a large formation of 109s coming in over the Channel. There were fifty of them. When our leader, a Canadian, gave the order to attack, I got on to the tail of four 109s at about 17,000 feet and attacked the outside one. After I had given him two short bursts of fire, he dived and crashed near Gravesend. When I looked around again the sky was full of Messerschmitt's, scattering in all directions. We chased them back to France and returned to our station for lunch. It seemed to me to be a pretty good mornings work.
>
> In the afternoon, we were sent up again and were told that there were some 109s off Selsey Bill. We saw them when were at about

> 20,000 feet. There were about forty of them at 500 feet above us. As they outnumbered us at about three to one, I suppose they thought they were on to a good thing. But in all events, they started to dive on us. We evaded their first attack and then turned on them. I picked on three, who had now made their way towards France. One was straggling a bit behind, I concentrated my fire on him and he went down in flames. The two other Messerschmitts had not seen me come up, so I closed up behind the leader and gave him a burst. As I did so the other 109 came up on my tail, but I held on to the fellow I had got.
>
> He must have been carrying a bomb, for after another burst from my guns he blew up before the one behind could protect him. There was nothing left of him in the sky that you could recognise as an aircraft, just a flash and a puff of smoke and bits of debris hurtling down all over the place. I must give that third Jerry pilot his due; he could have got away, but he stayed to fight. But the Spitfire's eight machine guns were too much for him and after a couple of turn; he went down in flames. Then I turned, found the squadron and returned home.

No. 92 Squadron lost one aircraft during a patrol on 17th November, when in combat with the enemy over Eastbourne, Sergeant Jack Allison had to force-land Spitfire N3229. The aircraft was written off due to the landing, but Allison walked away unscathed.

In action on 27th November, during the afternoon at 3.35 pm, Pilot Officer Peter Chesters of 74 Squadron was in combat over Chatham with Messerschmitts of JG51. In this engagement, his Spitfire P7306 was hit and he decided to take to his parachute after also being wounded in the leg. At this time, he noticed that his aircraft was over a village, so he remained in the cockpit long enough to steer it away, before jumping out. On landing, he was taken for treatment at the Orpington Hospital. His aircraft came to earth at Blacketts Marshes, near Sittingbourne.

During the afternoon of 28th November, six aircraft No. 66 Squadron took off at 2.50 pm led by Flight Lieutenant Bobby Oxspring and it was while the formation was climbing that the Spitfires of Pilot Officer Hubert 'Dizzy Allen and Sergeant Peter Willcocks accidently collided together damaging Willcocks tail-section, sending him into an inverted spin. Allen was fortunate enough to be able to take to his parachute, but Willcocks went down with his aircraft and was killed. Willcocks who came from South Croydon, had served firstly with No. 610 Squadron at Biggin Hill from 27th July 1940; he had then been posted to 66 Squadron at Kenley on 10th September, before returning once more to Biggin that November. His Spitfire P7491 coded LZ-K crashed at Marl Pit Hill, Hilders Lane, Edenbridge. Allen's aircraft P7492 LZ-F fell to earth on farmland at Upper Stonehurst Farm, Dormansland, Surrey.

Both Spitfires had been presentation aircraft funded by the City of Coventry Spitfire Fund, Willcock's aircraft being City of Coventry II and Allen's III. Hubert Allen would later recall the event and his subsequent bale-out:

> I had no alternative, but it was a very odd experience because it all happened very quickly as you can imagine, when somebody collides with you in mid-air. I stood on the seat and the wind blew me out; I was doing about 250 mph and so it was blowing a fair old hurricane. Going down you never seemed to move, you hung in mid-air, and you were stationary between heaven and hell.
>
> I was in fact I was over East Grinstead and the whole town was watching me because it was a Sunday and they had nothing better to do, the pubs weren't open yet. I finished up in a tree and was met by a posse of Home Guard with pitchforks; one of them had a shotgun which he pointed at my head. I managed to scramble down the tree and landed with a resounding thump from about ten feet. The old man said something to me in German, and I replied 'Shove off you stupid old whotsit,' and he replied 'blimey this one's an Englishman.' Yes I'm English,' I replied. Eventually I was picked up by car and driven back to Biggin.

The last day of November was to be a red letter day for No. 74 Squadron and the aerodrome. On that morning at 11.35 am, two Spitfires took of flown by Flight Lieutenant John Mungo Park and Pilot Officer H.M. Stephen and were given instructions to patrol a convoy near Deal, Kent. As they headed over the Thames Estuary the pilots were informed over the radio that a gaggle of eight Messerschmitt 109s were heading in from the south towards the vessels. Climbing up to 29,000 feet, they sighted the enemy formation and continued to climb their Spitfires to 34,000 feet to engage a single high-flying 109 acting as a 'weaver' Mungo-Park opened fire first from 150 yards and the enemy aircraft immediately dived causing Mungo-Park to overshoot.

Stephen then tried his luck and attacked, this time the 109 half-rolled, but Mungo Park followed it down firing a burst at 100-yards, causing the canopy of the enemy aircraft to fly off. He had to break away to avoid being in collision with the 109, which now received attention from Stephen once more. The German was now in a near vertical dive and was last seen going through cloud. Both pilots returned to Biggin and filed out their reports of the action.

Mungo-Park in his report noticed that the performance of his Spitfire Mk II at that height was quite manoeuvrable and as fast as a Messerschmitt 109 and that he found no difficulty in following the enemy aircraft. His Spitfire had been fitted with a newly developed half sheet of No-Mist to his cockpit front windscreen, which he considered excellent. The lower half of his windscreen froze completely at the height he was flying at, but the top half treated with No-Mist was completely clear and with that he was able to fire successfully and with no trouble. He stated it would be in his opinion to be an advantage if every aircraft was fitted with a complete sheet as soon as possible.

The Messerschmitt Bf109E-4 Werke No.(1145) they had shot down and in which they shared the victory, had been flown by Uffzoffizer F. Wagelin of 5/JG53, and crashed next to the Royal Military Canal at Ruckinge, near Ham Street, Kent. Wagelin had baled-out, but his parachute had damage to it and he died in hospital of his injuries sustained in the fall on 3rd December.

This aircraft had been the 600th enemy aircraft destroyed by a squadron based at Biggin Hill, and both Mungo Park and Stephen were placed in the public spotlight. The aerodrome was visited by Pathe News and the two pilots were interviewed before the cameras. The two minute feature was shown at all the cinemas around the country.

# December

Although weather conditions worsened during this month, the squadrons still remained active with patrols and intercepting German raids, when flying conditions allowed.

On 2nd December, both 66 and 74 Squadrons took off from the aerodrome at 11.00 am with 66 Squadron taking the lead. They were given instructions to patrol at 15,000 feet between the area of Dungeness and Dover to intercept a raid of thirty enemy aircraft which had been picked up flying at an altitude of 24,000 feet. Both the squadrons proceeded to climb and crossed the coast; 66 at 24,000 and 74 at 27,000 feet. No. 66 turned north and 74 south on sighting the groups of Messerschmitt 109s who were flying northwards on to their starboard side. The 109s continued past in a fast dive as 74 Squadron met them almost head-on.

The squadron then split up to attack. Squadron Leader 'Sailor' Malan positioned himself on to the tail of one of the 109s, which had turned south-east into the sun and was flying flat out to escape. Malan opened fire whilst diving down at 500 yards and closed into within 100 yards. He observed smoke to pour heavily from the enemy machine which flatted out from its dive at 1,000 feet and pulled up into the sun, then slowed down. Malan continued to follow and fired another burst from his guns, he saw the 109s canopy hood fly off and what appeared to be a dinghy, flash past him. The 109 slowly turned on to its back and went into the sea inverted. It was believed that the pilot was dead or unable to get out of his aircraft which crashed 10-miles off Dungeness.

On return to Biggin Hill, 74 Squadron claimed three 109s destroyed, one probably destroyed and one damaged without casualties to

themselves.
A signal of congratulations was received at the aerodrome from Headquarters No. 11 Group at Uxbridge and also from the Secretary of State for Air Sir Archibald Sinclair who wrote:

> Please convey my congratulations to 74 Squadron on their brilliant fighting over the last four weeks, during which my records show that they have had the destruction of 35 enemy aircraft confirmed and have only lost two machines themselves. This is a splendid achievement.

It was during this month that another Biggin Hill legend began. A simple piece of wood panel painted up for the use as a black-out screen at the White Hart Pub was to become a permanent memorial to those that had flown from the aerodrome. During the middle part of December, Group Captain Grice, the station commander was given notice that after two years he was to be replaced; his position was to be taken over by Group Captain F.O. Soden DFC.

As Christmas approached, a farewell party was organised by his fellow officers and pilots for a special send-off at the White Hart. As the party drew to a close, Richard Grice chalked up his name on the black-out board which was hanging near the bar door. Having written his signature, he asked for the rest of the officers to add their names to the board. So the legend of the board began. Throughout the remainder of the war other pilots added their signatures.

When peace came in 1945, the Landlady Kath Preston and her husband Teddy decided to have the board framed with glass to protect the valuable signatures. An unveiling party was organised and those that had survived the war were invited to attend. It was decided that 'Sailor' Malan would have the honour of the unveiling that day. The Biggin Hill board can still be viewed by visiting the Shoreham Aircraft Museum in Shoreham Village in Kent. As for Richard Grice, on his departure from the aerodrome, he was first carried through the Officers' Mess on the shoulders of some of his pilots to a rousing cheer. His new posting would be to Australia.

Although the reconstruction of the aerodrome had been underway for over a month, the living conditions for the personnel were still very basic, so much so that Group Captain Soden decided to write a letter of complaint to the Secretary of State for Air, Sir Archibald Sinclair. In his letter he stated 'I have just taken over at Biggin Hill and the chaps are living under conditions of unnecessary filth and squalor. In fact, if ever has so little been done for those few who have done so much!'

During the early morning of 29th December a patrol was sent off at 9.45 am consisting of two Spitfires from No. 66 Squadron flown by Flight Lieutenant G.P. Christie and Pilot Officer P. Oliver; they were given instructions to patrol a line between Dungeness and Dover. It was during this patrol that at approximately 10.15 am that both pilots sighted a single Dornier 17 bomber probably on a reconnaissance mission near Dungeness, flying at a height of 3,500 feet. Flight Lieutenant Christie's combat report gives the story of what happened:

> We took off from Biggin Hill at 9.45 hours and whilst approaching Dungeness I saw single Dornier 17 flying 2-miles out to sea at 3, 500 feet. I climbed to attack and opened fire with a 2-second burst at 200 yards and then circled around delivering deflection burst from both above and below the enemy aircraft plus both sides, finally closing to point blank range. I saw the lower rear gunner lolling in his cockpit obviously dead. I had to break off the engagement as I had run out of ammunition. I returned to base, where I landed at 10.30 hours. My plane was hit three times by enemy fire, but was not damaged.

Both pilots had delivered attacks on the German aircraft, but lost it when it entered cloud in mid-Channel; they claimed it as damaged, having no proof that it had crashed into the sea.

So ended a dramatic year in RAF Biggin Hill's history, it had witnessed the threat of the Nazi invasion and it had been halted. Britain was now the sole keeper of the flame of freedom in Western Europe and the hope of those occupied countries, that one day the tide would turn against Hitler. In the year that followed Biggin Hill would play a major part in bringing the war back across the Channel as RAF Fighter and Bomber Command began to launch offensive operations against the enemy? Wing formations of three to five fighter squadrons would now escort the bombers over France, Belgium and Holland targeting German installations, airfields and troops. Thus in early 1941 the Biggin Hill Wing came into being. It would be another four long hard years to final victory.

# Bibliography

The following books are recommended by the author as essential background reading for those interested in RAF Biggin Hill and RAF campaigns of 1940

*Aces High*, Christopher Shores & Clive Williams, Grub Street, London 1994
*Air Battle Dunkirk*, Norman Franks, Grub Street, London 2000
*Battle of Britain Then & Now,* Winston Ramsey, After the Battle Publications 1980
*Battle of France Then & Now*, Peter D. Cornwell, After the Battle Publications 2007
*Biggin on the Bump*, Bob Ogley, Froglets Publications 1990
*Fighter Command's Sergeant Aces of 1940*, Richard C. Smith, Mitor Publications 2007
*Ghosts of Biggin Hill*, Bob Ogley, Froglets Publications 2001
*Hurricane Squadron Ace*, Nick Thomas, Pen & Sword Aviation 2014
*Men of the Battle of Britain*, Ken Wynn, CCB Associates 1999
*Pure Chance*, Dame Felicity Peake, Airlife Publishing Limited 1993
*RAF Biggin Hill*, Graham Wallace, Putnam & Co. Limited 1957
*Scramble- A narrative history of the Battle of Britain*, Norman Gelb, Michael Joseph Ltd 1986
*Sky Spy*, Ray Holmes, Airlife Publishing Ltd 1989

RAF Squadron Operation Record Books & Combat Reports – National Archive, Kew, London

| | | |
|---|---|---|
| No. 3 Squadron | Air 27/32 | |
| No. 25 Squadron | Air 27/308 | |
| No. 32 Squadron | Air 27/360 | Air 50/16 |
| No. 66 Squadron | Air 27/598 | Air 50/26 |
| No. 72 Squadron | Air 27/624 | Air 50/30 |

| | | |
|---|---|---|
| No. 74 Squadron | Air 27/640 | Air 50/32 |
| No. 79 Squadron | Air 27/664 | Air 50/33 |
| No. 92 Squadron | Air 27/915 | Air 50/40 |
| No. 111Squadron | Air 27/866 | |
| No. 141 Squadron | Air 27/969 | Air 50/61 |
| No. 213 Squadron | Air 27/1315 | Air 50/83 |
| No. 229 Squadron | Air 27/1418 | Air 50/86 |
| No. 242 Squadron | Air 27/1471 | Air 50/92 |
| No. 263 Squadron | Air 27/263 | |
| No. 601 Squadron | Air 27/2067 | |
| No. 610 Squadron | Air 27/2106 | Air 50/172 |

Imperial War Museum Sound Archive Pilot interviews

| | |
|---|---|
| Air Commodore Peter Brothers Ref | Ref No. 10218 |
| Squadron Leader Douglas Grice | Ref No. 10871 |
| Squadron Leader Tony Bartley | Ref No. 11086 |
| Group Captain Brian Kingcome | Ref No. 10152 |
| Wing Commander Don Kingaby | Ref No. 02276/E |
| Squadron Leader Roger Frankland | Ref No. 10182 |
| Squadron Leader Cyril Bamberger | Ref No. 27074 |
| Group Captain George Johns | Ref No. 11616 |

# INDEX

**Personnel**

# INDEX

# INDEX

# INDEX

# INDEX

# INDEX

# INDEX

# INDEX

**General - Place Names**

# INDEX

# INDEX

# INDEX

# INDEX

# INDEX



**RAF Aerodromes & Operational Training Units etc**

# INDEX

# AUTHOR

Richard C. Smith was born in London and became interested in military and aviation history at an early age. Since 2000, he has written twelve books, six of which were published by the renowned Grub Street Publishers. These included four tomes covering the history of his local famous aerodrome of RAF Hornchurch. In 2007, Richard published independently with Mitor Publications. Apart from writing, he has been involved in helping with research for TV documentaries, which included 'Two Men in a Trench' and 'Britain's Flying Past.' He also attends heritage and air show events with his RAF Hornchurch & Battle of Britain Roadshow exhibition.